READINGS IN ST. JOHN'S GOSPEL

READINGS

IN

ST. JOHN'S GOSPEL

(SECOND SERIES: CHAPTERS XIII–XXI)

BY

WILLIAM TEMPLE

ARCHBISHOP OF YORK

MACMILLAN AND CO., LIMITED
ST. MARTIN'S STREET, LONDON
1940

COPYRIGHT

PREFACE

This Second Series of *Readings in St. John's Gospel* includes all the chapters after that with which the First Series closed. I need not here repeat my expression of indebtedness to commentators and other writers. The same authors have been my chief guides.

For the convenience of those who read this Series without having read the First Series, the Introduction to the whole is reprinted in this volume.

But I must renew my thanks to Canon Baker who has once more read all the proofs, and to my wife who has read the whole in typescript and has helped me with many suggestions for making clearer the movement of thought. I also want to thank Miss Howell-Thomas who typed almost the whole of the manuscript.

WILLIAM EBOR:

Bishopthorpe, York
October 1939

TO

THE MEMORY OF

JOHN LEOFRIC STOCKS

CONTENTS

ACT III

ACT IV

ACT V

EPILOGUE

Merciful Lord, we beseech thee to cast thy bright beams of light upon thy Church, that it, being enlightened by the doctrine of thy blessed Apostle and Evangelist Saint John, may so walk in the light of thy truth that it may at length attain to the light of everlasting life ; through Jesus Christ our Lord.

INTRODUCTION

THIS book is not a systematic commentary or exposition; nor is it intended for scholars or theologians — though whatever value it has for souls on pilgrimage may be as real for them as for others. Again, it is not a series of devotional meditations, though it contains some of these. It has no distinctive and consistent character. But it is an attempt to share with any who read it what I find to be my own thoughts as I read the profoundest of all writings.

Consequently it is not chiefly concerned with the question what the writer consciously intended, though of course that question frequently arises; nor again with the question how much of what is here set down has its origin in the deeds and words of the Lord Jesus when on earth, though of that something is said later in this Introduction. I am chiefly concerned with what arises in my mind and spirit as I read; and I hope this is not totally different from saying that I am concerned with what the Holy Spirit says to me through the Gospel.

This is always a legitimate way to read the Bible, and religiously the most important. For the Word of God does not consist of printed propositions; it is living; it is personal; it is Jesus Christ. That living Word of God speaks to us through the printed words of Scripture; and all our study of those printed words helps us to receive it. But the point of vital importance is the utterance of the Divine Word to the soul, the self-communication of the Father to His children. The Fourth Gospel is written with full consciousness of that truth, and so a method, always legitimate and always spiritually valuable, is here almost obligatory. Why this should be so will become clear as we consider the questions of authorship and historical reliability so far as it is relevant to these " readings " to do so.

AUTHORSHIP

It would be quite out of place to discuss in this Introduction the vexed question of the authorship of the Fourth Gospel. The literature of the subject is immense. But it is relevant to set down without argument what my own limited study of the question has led me to believe.

First, I regard as self-condemned any theory which fails to find a very close connexion between the Gospel and John the son of Zebedee. The combination of external and internal evidence is overwhelming on this point. For the external evidence reference may be made to Westcott's classical commentary, and, for the internal evidence, to that and to Scott Holland's brilliant lectures.[1] Scott Holland conclusively proves (as I think) the Apostolic authority of the Gospel. Until recently I held that the balance of evidence was in favour of Westcott's view that John the Apostle actually dictated the book. But the references to John the Elder, as some one distinct from the Apostle, cannot be set aside, and the view which now seems to me to do fullest justice to the evidence is that the writer — the Evangelist — is John the Elder, who was an intimate disciple of John the Apostle; that he records the teaching of that Apostle with great fidelity; that the Apostle is the " Witness ", to whom reference is sometimes made, and is also the " disciple whom Jesus loved ".

It may be that the Apostle actually dictated to the Elder parts of what now constitutes the Gospel; I incline to think so; but parts are the Elder's own recollection of the Apostle's teaching and parts are his own comment. By adopting this view we can recognise

[1] *The Fourth Gospel.*

that the author of the First Epistle is also the actual
writer of the Fourth Gospel, while also admitting the
differences to which Professor Dodd and others have
called attention. The Epistles are the work of John
the Elder in every sense of the words. They exhibit
a smaller vocabulary, and in some respects a more
crystallised outlook and greater tendency to definition,
than the Gospel of which the Elder is the writer but
the Apostle is the true author.

It is not possible to say which sections of the Gospel
come direct from the Apostle; but I am sure that we
are nearer the truth in maximising than in minimising
these.

Historical Reliability

(1) *As regards the Course of Events*

There is a marked contrast between the outline of
the Gospel story as recorded by the Synoptists and
the outline presented by St. John. The events of the
Synoptic narrative, until the Triumphal Entry, take
place mainly in Galilee or on the journey from Galilee
to Jerusalem; the events of the Johannine narrative
take place mainly in Jerusalem. The Synoptic narrative appears to occupy one year only; the Johannine
covers three Passovers (ii, 13; v, 1; xii, 1). The
dates given for the Last Supper and the Crucifixion
are apparently different. These and other such considerations have led many in the past to throw doubt
on the reliability of the Fourth Gospel. But closer
study leads to a different conclusion. For the fact is
that the Synoptists provide no chronology of the
ministry at all until the last week; we do not have to
choose between two incompatible chronologies for the
Johannine chronology is the only one that we have.
Further, the Synoptic narrative is unintelligible unless
something like the Johannine story is accepted. How
was it possible for the Lord to plan the preparations

for the Triumphal Entry and for the Last Supper if
He had never been to Jerusalem since boyhood, or
had had no opportunity of gaining adherents there?
What is meant by the bitter cry over the city " How
often would I have gathered thy children!" (*St. Matthew* xxiii, 37; *St. Luke* xiii, 34) unless there had been
missionary enterprises in it on more occasions than one?

Modern commentators mostly accept the Johannine
dates for the Last Supper and Crucifixion, on general
grounds of probability. The Synoptists retain a recollection of this date in the saying attributed to the
Chief Priests, " Not on the feast day, lest there be an
uproar among the people ", which harmonises ill with
their record of an arrest apparently carried out on the
feast day itself.[1]   St. John put the arrest earlier, so
that the Lord was condemned and crucified on the
Day of Preparation, the day on which the Paschal
Lamb was killed; and then, of course, the Last Supper
was not the actual Passover, but rather a fellowship
meal with evident paschal associations.

Moreover it is well to remember that where there
is a divergence between the Synoptists and St. John,
it is not a case of three witnesses against one; for in
this respect St. Mark governs the Synoptic tradition;
the first and third Gospels rely on the second for such
a framework of order as they display. The divergence
then is between the Second Gospel and the Fourth.
Now St. Mark wrote his recollection of the teaching
and preaching of St. Peter, and the scheme of his
Gospel may be represented by saying that it is a
narrative of the Passion with an introduction. If we
accept this, and also recognise that St. Mark does not
even purport to provide a chronological scheme, we
must agree that the evidence to be set against the very
clear and full chronological scheme provided by St.
John is negligible.

[1] But the Synoptists are not explicit as regards the date, and it is possible
to interpret them as agreeing with St. John.

We have thus disposed of the main ground for questioning the historical reliability of the Fourth Gospel as a record of events.[1] But it may still be asked how far the author is really concerned with historical facts. He plainly avows his motive in xx, 31. He does not profess to give a complete record; he selects from among abundant material; and he does this with a deliberate purpose: " these are written that ye may believe that Jesus is the Christ, the Son of God, and that believing ye may have life in his name ".

It is no doubt true that St. John selects his chosen events for record because of their significance; but it is essential for his purpose that the significant occasion should also be an event. If the whole story is a myth its quality as revelation is destroyed. The Gospel is that " the Word was made flesh ", and being incarnate so spoke, so acted, so died and so rose from death. It is not the mere occurrence of its several episodes that constitutes the Gospel; it is their spiritual and eternal significance; but part of their spiritual and eternal significance is their physical and temporal occurrence. For it is the whole world, inclusive of matter — of flesh and blood — which God so loved that He gave His only begotten Son.

It is then vital to St. John's purpose that the events which he records should be actual events. We can be quite sure that he never consciously wrote what he did not believe to be fact; he is not a constructor of allegories. And we have already seen reason for thinking that the very points which have led some to doubt his reliability as a witness are in fact grounds for confidence in it. We shall read the Gospel as valid history so far as its record of events is concerned.

(2) As regards the Discourses

Can the same confidence be placed in the record

---

[1] About the special problem presented by the Raising of Lazarus something will be said when that point of the narrative is reached. See p. 175.

of our Lord's discourses, which fills so large a part of the whole Gospel? The answer to that question calls for some preliminary reflections.

(*a*) The discourses recorded in the Synoptic Gospels are mostly such as were delivered to " the multitudes " or to the local religious leaders in Galilee. Those recorded in the Fourth Gospel are mostly such as were delivered in controversy with the religious leaders in Jerusalem, or in intimate converse with the inner group of the disciples. It is natural that there should be a broad difference alike of subject-matter and of manner.

(*b*) The consideration just mentioned goes far to account for the note of sharper division and even of harshness in the Johannine account — as for example in Chapter VIII. But much depends on the way in which the crucial passages are read. For example, the stern words about the spiritual paternity of " the Jews " in viii, 31-47 can be, and should be, read in the tone of sad recognition of a fact, not of personal irritation. I see no reason here to doubt that the Lord really spoke very much as is recorded.

(*c*) It is in the light of these considerations that we may meet the complaint that in this Gospel the Lord is presented as self-assertive. Certainly we must admit that if the claims which He here makes are not true they are intolerably arrogant. If He is a very good man completely surrendered to the Spirit of God, He cannot, without offence, speak as the Johannine Christ speaks. But if He is God come in the flesh He not only may, He must proclaim Himself as the fount of salvation. Love, not self-concern, demands that He should call men to Himself as alone the revelation of the Father. At the same time it is appropriate that He should do this either when He is expressly challenged, as the religious leaders at Jerusalem challenged Him, or in conversation with His intimate disciples; and it is precisely in these circumstances that the Fourth Gospel presents Him as making these claims.

They are not altogether absent from the Synoptic narrative, but they are naturally less prominent in that record of ministry among the Galilean fisher-folk and peasants.

If, when all is said, any still feel a trace of self-assertion in the sense which involves moral defect, it may be held that the Evangelist has imported into his record of what the Lord said some of his own devoted eagerness. But I find no reason for recourse to such a plea. Those who admit, and wish to proclaim, all that the Lord is here represented as saying about Himself, will feel gratitude, not resentment, that the words are recorded; those who do not admit their truth are bound to resent, or at least to regret, their presence in this profoundly sympathetic presentation of the Lord.

(d) What is meant by the question " Did the Lord say this? " The word " say " is not so simple as it looks. It may mean the utterance of certain sounds; it may mean the conveyance of certain meanings. If we take it in the former sense no doubt the Synoptists are the more accurate recorders of what they narrate; if we take it in the latter sense I should claim that St. John is the more accurate recorder.

It is commonly found that those sermons which most profoundly stir their hearers are comparatively insipid when read " in cold print "; and those which are most moving to read were comparatively ineffectual in delivery. The atmosphere of conviction generated by the great preacher is due to his whole personality rather than to the words used, and the sermons for which we are most grateful are those which help us to believe vitally what we knew quite well before the sermon started. My father, who was described by one who knew him as " granite on fire " and was certainly never regarded as sentimental, could not speak of the love of God without tears. His Good Friday sermons are still stirring to read; but they are not what they were to those who felt, as they listened, the impact of

his passionate conviction. The exact record of the
words spoken cannot carry that; but a great artist
might do much to convey it, and, by re-writing the
sermon, give a truer record of it.

Let us take another illustration. A good photograph is vastly preferable to a bad portrait. But the
great portrait painter may give a representation of a
man which no photographer can emulate. And he
does it by drawing what is not at any moment altogether
actual. The Synoptists may give us something more
like the perfect photograph; St. John gives us the
more perfect portrait.

And he does this, as every artist must, by letting
his mind and his subject interpenetrate one another
and then expressing the result. We are not likely of
ourselves to come closer to the Lord by exercising our
coarse faculties upon the more exact record of words
spoken and deeds done than by entering into communion of thought and feeling with the mind of that
disciple who lay " breast to breast with God ".

There is a truth of general import which is relevant
here. Christ wrote no book; he left in the world as
His witness a " body " of men and women upon whom
His Spirit came. There was to be nothing stereotyped.
The living society — the Church — was to be the
primary witness. The Gospels were written by
members of the Church for their fellow-members, and
each is " The Gospel according to " somebody. What
reaches us is never a certified record but always a
personal impression. Thus our concern is always with
the Christ of faith, not with some supposed different
Jesus of history. It is by the faith of others that our
faith is kindled, even when that other is a Synoptic
Evangelist. And this is true to the whole purpose and
method of Christ in His mission. Had it been otherwise, the movement of the Spirit might have been
fettered; but now it is free. Yet in the wisdom of God
there come to us two kinds of personal impression —

both that which is more akin to the photograph and that which is more akin to the portrait. And each illuminates the other.

(e) Because St. John is the portrait-painter, consciously submitting his mind to be interpenetrated by his subject, and then giving forth what his mind contains, he is not careful to distinguish between what the Lord historically " said " and what that saying has come to mean for him in his lifelong meditation.

> What first were guessed as points, I now knew stars,
> And named them in the Gospel I have writ.

So speaks St. John in Browning's poem *A Death in the Desert*, which remains the most penetrating interpretation of St. John that exists in the English language.

Thus a historical conversation may be coloured by a later experience, as in iv, 38 where the words " I sent you to reap that whereon ye have not laboured " refers rather to later experience than to a mission already launched at the time of the conversation with the Woman of Samaria. It is important to remember that the convention of historical writing in the ancient world approved the attribution to leading personages of speeches expressing what was known to be their view in a form which is due to the historian. In such compositions key-phrases actually spoken would naturally be recorded.

We may sometimes feel sure that this saying or that was uttered by the Lord as it is recorded; but it would be, I think, a mistake to look for original and authentic utterances as each the nucleus of a discourse. It is Jesus who speaks — Jesus who is " the same yesterday and to-day and for ever " — whether in the flesh or in the experience of His beloved disciple. And we have to remember that when St. John records a promise made by our Lord he does so not only because the promise was made but because it is fulfilled. When St. John records the words " I will not

b

leave you desolate; I come to you " (xiv, 16) their value is not only that this, or something fairly represented by this, was uttered, but that the thing described has happened.

This fusion of the purely historical with the spiritual is part of the character and meaning of this Gospel, which is not purely historical, nor in the proper sense mystical, but in the completest possible degree sacramental. Each conversation or discourse contained in the Gospel actually took place. But it is so reported as to convey, not only the sounds uttered or the meaning then apprehended, but the meaning which, always there, has been disclosed by lifelong meditation. Thus I am convinced that conversations with Nicodemus and with a Samaritan woman at Jacob's Well actually occurred, and followed substantially the course of our record. But the record, while obviously condensing the original by reducing it to its own analysis or synopsis, yet presents it in the literary style of the Evangelist rather than of the Lord. It is worthy of notice, incidentally, that the conversation with Nicodemus, having been heard by the Beloved Disciple, has become part of his own experience, and therefore passes over into comment at a quite uncertain point, whereas the conversation with the Woman of Samaria, of which the Lord Himself must (one supposes) have given the digest to the disciples on their return, appears without any appended comment.

So, to take another illustration, I am sure that the Lord said, as they crossed the Temple Court with the Golden Vine full in view, " I am the true Vine " (xv, 1). This carries within it, by implication, all that follows. But when later He is recorded as also saying " Apart from me ye can do nothing " (xv, 5) this is a record as much of the disciples' experience as of the Lord's utterance: but it is the record not only of an empirical impotence, but of a divine assurance, like that which came to St. Paul — " My grace is sufficient

INTRODUCTION xix

for thee; for my power is made perfect in weakness "
(*II Corinthians* xii, 9).

Thus, by the passage of the old remembered words
and deeds through the experience, thought and adoring
love of the disciple, we are helped to a knowledge of
Christ which is not " after the flesh " but " after the
spirit " (*II Corinthians* v, 16). In the historical life we
behold the eternal glory.

We shall read the Gospel, then, in order to enter
into the Evangelist's and the Beloved Disciple's communion with the Lord, not asking at each point precisely what was spoken or done, but knowing that as
we share the experience, historical and spiritual, from
which the Gospel flows we shall come nearer to the
heart and mind of Jesus our Lord than ever our own
minds could bring us by meditation upon the precise
words that He uttered.

(*f*) The same reason which leads St. John to record
the words of the Lord in the form expressive of their
significance as that has become clear to him permits
him also, as we have noticed, to pass from the record
to his own comment upon it without any indication of
the transition. There is a clear instance of this in
Chapter III after the conversation with Nicodemus. I
do not think this calls for any further discussion here,
but consonantly with what has already been said, I
think we are wise to regard all that we can as utterance
of the Lord in the sense described, and to put the point
of transition to comment on the part of either the
Beloved Disciple (the Witness) or the Evangelist as
late in the text as possible.

Some General Considerations

(1) The Gospel is through and through Palestinian.
The notion that it is in any sense Hellenistic is contrary
to its whole tenour. It is set in all the vivid concrete
scenery of the actual Ministry in Palestine. What

Hellenist could, or would, have written Chapter IX?
And this is no more than a specially clear instance of
an all-pervasive character. The whole idea of a Hellenistic quality comes from the Prologue. But this,
too, is essentially Jewish, though the term " Logos "
is used in its Hellenistic as well as its Jewish sense,
as a medium of interpretation to the Greek-speaking
people of Ephesus. The Prologue bears evident traces
of a mind accustomed to think in Aramaic, even if we
consider that Dr. Burney failed to establish the case
for an Aramaic original afterwards translated into
Greek. After the close of the Prologue the term Logos
does not recur. The thought which it was used to
introduce — that the historical life and death and
resurrection of Jesus Christ is a self-utterance of the
Eternal God, so that in the temporal event we behold
the eternal reality — governs the whole Gospel. But
this is neither Jewish nor Greek; it is specifically
Christian. A partly Greek term was used to introduce
this truth to minds formed by Greek culture, and was
then used no more. With St. John as truly as with
St. Mark we accompany the Lord in Galilee and in
Jerusalem, and breathe the air of Palestine.

(2) In the proper sense of the word " mystical ",
as signifying a direct apprehension of God by the
human mind, St. John is strongly anti-mystical. But
he is even more strongly sacramental. He is emphatic
that " no man hath beheld God at any time " (i, 18);[1]
that saying repudiates the essentially mystical experience; but he is equally emphatic that " God only
begotten hath declared him ". In the great affirmation that " the Word became flesh and we beheld his
glory " (i, 14) is implicit a whole theory of the relation
between spirit and matter. Christianity is the most
materialistic of all great religions. The others hope to
achieve spiritual reality by ignoring matter — calling

[1] The possibility that these words only mean that God is invisible is
ruled out by vi, 46, where there cannot be any reference to physical vision.

it illusion (*maya*) or saying that it does not exist; the
result is a failure to control the physical side of life, a
lofty religious philosophy side by side with sensual in-
dulgence, not indeed in the same persons but in the
same religious tradition. Christianity, based as it is
on the Incarnation, regards matter as destined to be
the vehicle and instrument of spirit, and spirit as fully
actual so far as it controls and directs matter.

Thus the appointed Sacraments of the Church are
not something unrelated to all other human experience;
some have wished to treat them so, with a view to a
greater reverence for them; but the result is an inclina-
tion towards magic, and an evisceration of the Sacraments by elimination of their ethical content. The
Sacraments of the Church are appointed means of
grace wherein the Lord of the Church makes use,
for His central purpose, of the character implanted
by Him in the constitution of the universe as a
whole. They represent and focus a principle at work
far beyond themselves. It is no accident that the discourses in the Fourth Gospel which contain references
to Baptism and the Eucharist are recorded in complete detachment from the practice or institution of
either.

(3) One marked characteristic of the mind of the
Evangelist, or of the Beloved Disciple, is worth mention. He often records argument in debate, but he
does not argue from premises to conclusions as a
method of apprehending truth. Rather he puts
together the various constituent parts of truth and
contemplates them in their relations to one another.
Thus he seems to say " look at A; now look at B;
now at A B; now at C; now at B C; now at A C;
now at D and E; now at A B E; now at C E ", and
so on in any variety of combination that facilitates new
insight. It is the method of artistic, as distinct from
scientific, apprehension, and is appropriate to truth
which is in no way dependent on, or derived from,

other truth, but makes its own direct appeal to reason, heart and conscience.

THE JOHANNINE AND SYNOPTIST PICTURE
OF CHRIST

A Gospel is essentially a proclamation of the good news concerning God and His Kingdom which is offered to men in Christ, in whom " God hath visited and redeemed his people ". The question of greatest importance that can be asked concerning it is this: Is it the true picture of Christ?

It has been said that the picture in the Synoptic Gospels and the picture in the Fourth Gospel are incompatible, and that we have to choose between them. So far as this contention is based on difference in the record of facts, or on the matter or manner of the Lord's speech, we have dealt with it already. Broadly speaking, there is no incompatibility in the record of facts, though there are some points at which adjustment is difficult — e.g. the Cleansing of the Temple — and one, the Raising of Lazarus, where it is supremely difficult. Something will be said of these in their own place. But, speaking generally, the truth is that the Synoptic narrative is unintelligible without the narrative of St. John. Far from being incompatible with the former the latter is necessary to it.

As regards the " style " of the discourses, the character of the Johannine record has been discussed. No one suggests that a phonographic record would have retained from the utterance of the Lord the sounds which we make as we read the Fourth Gospel aloud, or even their Aramaic counterpart. What is maintained is that the themes were actually handled by the Lord, and that this Gospel gives to us what His utterance was afterwards known to have contained.

This gives rise to one special source of complexity.

The relation of the Beloved Disciple or of the Evangelist to the Lord was at the date of dictation or of writing that of a worshipper to his God. This, too, is read back into the old story. It depicts the disciples as conscious of His Messiahship and His Deity, because they are now conscious of it, and the spiritual meaning of what was said in Jerusalem or Galilee is partly derived from the divine status of the Speaker. And this has probably coloured, as later experience has throughout coloured, the form given to the utterance. Our generation, with its eagerness to get back to " what actually happened " should begin with the Synoptic narrative, and there watch the dawn and growth of apprehension. But " what actually happened " is not — was not — the real occurrence, for it did not of itself disclose the supremely important fact that the words were spoken and the deeds done by God Incarnate. So the Fourth Gospel brings us nearer to the reality — the " substance " — of what happened.

History is always involved in ambiguity at this point, because fact and interpretation cannot be disentangled. If I say " Charles Stuart was executed ", that is true, but not the whole truth. I add something if I say " King Charles I was executed ". I add a good deal more if I say " King Charles I was martyred ". The new term is interpretative; but if the interpretation is true the statement is historically true. Yet it requires other than historical categories to justify it.

So if it had been said to the shepherds " A baby is born in Bethlehem " it would have been true, but only part of the truth. If it had been said " A baby is born who will be called Jesus by divine command " that also would have been true, and evidence for what was understood to be a divine command would have been available. Such evidence could never amount to historical proof that God gave that command; but if He did, that, too, is historical fact. The statement " To you is born a Saviour which is Christ the Lord " uses categories of which History knows nothing; yet if it is true at all, it is historically true.

It is in an analogous manner that the Fourth Gospel leads us to the heart of facts whose merely " actual " aspect did not fully exhibit this full reality.

But the question is raised on deeper grounds. When all is allowed for, Is the Johannine Christ the same person as the Synoptic Christ? Has He the same outlook on the world? Has He the same conception of His own relation to God? and of His mission in the world?

Two prejudices have in the past obscured this question. In the later nineteenth century there was a tendency to suppose that " the Jesus of History " must have been a purely human and non-supernatural person; and this was believed in spite of the fact that, admittedly, the earliest of the four Gospels, St. Mark's, is crowded with miracles. It was held that the simple preacher of love towards God and man could be discerned behind the Marcan, Lucan and Matthaean narratives. (Why anyone should have troubled to crucify the Christ of Liberal Protestantism has always been a mystery.) But this view is now almost everywhere abandoned. It is now recognised that the only Christ for whose existence there is any evidence at all is a miraculous Figure making stupendous claims. These would naturally be less prominent in narratives of the Galilean ministry than in a narrative of controversy with the ecclesiastical leaders in Jerusalem. But they are there, and from the earliest and best of our strands of evidence — the document or tradition on which the First and Third Gospels draw, commonly called Q — comes a saying purely " Johannine " in quality: " All things have been delivered unto me of my Father; and no one knoweth the Son save the Father, neither doth any know the Father save the Son, and he to whomsoever the Son willeth to reveal Him " (*St. Matthew* xi, 27; cf. *St. Luke* x, 22).

The other prejudice dies harder. It is to the effect
that the Lord was deeply affected by an " apocalyptic "
outlook, and anticipated His own return in glory at an
early though unknown date.   This, it is urged, is the
Synoptic picture; and the situation disclosed in the
early chapters of the *Acts of the Apostles* corresponds to
this.   On the other hand, St. John, writing when the
great transition in thought had been effected and there
was no longer expectation of an early " return ", sub-
stitutes the discourse on the coming of the Paraclete
for the apocalypse of *St. Mark* xiii and the corresponding passages in *St. Matthew* and *St. Luke*.   It is
recognised that St. John has an outlook peculiar among
writers of the New Testament, though the later
Pauline Epistles approach it.   This finds its focus in
the conviction that the divine glory, which we behold
throughout the life of Christ, is most fully expressed
in His Passion.   But this is commonly regarded as
part of a profound readjustment of thought in the
light of the fuller experience of the Church.

We must candidly admit that the view thus traced
to the Synoptists is certainly that at which the Apostles
had arrived at the time of the speeches recorded in the
Acts of the Apostles as having been made by St. Peter
on the feast of Pentecost and in the immediately following period.   It represents what the first disciples
at that date supposed the Lord to have said and meant.
None the less I maintain that the Synoptic record
itself discloses as the real mind of the Lord what
St. John first makes clear.   St. Peter and St. Mark
probably held the outlook which these critics attribute
both to them and to the Lord Himself; yet their
reproduction of His own teaching shows that they had
not fully understood Him, and that He was in historical
fact what St. John for the first time set forth.

Every great man is greater than his followers at
first appreciate; it is posterity by which he is truly
understood.   And every original genius is hampered

by the terms which contemporary language offers as
the necessary and sole medium of his self-expression.
He must take the best terms available, and trust that
his special use of them will gradually correct the suggestions attaching to them, which are alien from his
thought, until at last he has imposed his own meaning
on them. So the Lord used the language of apocalyptic for certain of His purposes; so He accepted the
title of Messiah, though He never took the initiative in
using it of Himself. It was full of suggestions bearing
no relation to what He had to do; yet it was the best
term available, and it was far more true to say that He
was the promised Messiah than to deny it; for to
Him was entrusted the essential task of the Messiah —
to inaugurate the Kingdom of God.

My contention is that there is no incompatibility
between the Synoptic and the Johannine portraits,
because the Synoptic portrait is substantially Johannine.
In support of this contention I offer an outline-sketch
of the Synoptic portrait. Many of the points included
in it will also be recalled in their appropriate places in
the Johannine story.

The Lord, at His Baptism, is conscious of the call
to begin now the work of Messiah: the voice from
heaven — " This is " (*or* " Thou art ") " my beloved
Son in whom I am well pleased " — undoubtedly
carries this meaning. At once, therefore, He goes into
solitude to consider what manner of Messiah He shall
be. The story of the Temptations is, of course, a
parable of His spiritual wrestlings, told by Himself to
His disciples. It represents the rejection, under three
typical forms, of all existing conceptions of the Messianic task, which was to inaugurate the Kingdom of
God. Should He use the power with which, as
Messiah, He is endowed to satisfy the creature wants
of Himself and His human brethren, so fulfilling the
hope of a " good time coming " which prophets had
presented in the picture of the Messianic Banquet —

(cf. e.g. *Isaiah* xxv, 6)? Should He be a Caesar-Christ, winning the Kingdoms of the world and the glory of them by establishing an earthly monarchy and ruling from the throne of David in perfect righteousness — (cf. e.g. *Isaiah* ix, 6, 7)? Should He provide irresistible evidence of His divine mission, appearing in the Temple courts upborne by angels, so that doubt would be impossible — (cf. e.g. *Daniel* vii, 13, 14, and *Enoch*)? Every one of these conceptions contained truth. When men are obedient to the Kingdom of God and His justice, everyone will have what he needs for food and clothing (*St. Matthew* vi, 33). The Kingdom of God is the realm of perfect justice where God's righteous will is done (*St. Matthew* vi, 10). The authority of Christ is absolute and can claim the support of the hosts of heaven (*St. Matthew* xxviii, 18; xxvi, 53). Yet if any or all of these are taken as fully representative of the Kingdom and its inauguration they have one fatal defect. They all represent ways of securing the outward obedience of men apart from inward loyalty; they are ways of controlling conduct, but not ways of controlling hearts and wills. He might bribe men to obey Him by the promise of good things, and so encourage man's evil tendency to care more for creature comforts than for the Word of God. He might coerce men to obey by threat of penalty, as earthly rulers do, and so Himself worship, and encourage men to worship, the Prince of this world. He might offer irresistible proof so that men would have to think the Gospel true even if they wished that it were not, putting to the proof the God who claims men's trust. In other words, all the rejected methods are essentially appeals to self-interest; and the Kingdom of God, who is Love, cannot be established in that way.

He has stripped Messiahship bare, repudiating all existing conceptions of it. Only the essential task remains — to inaugurate the Kingdom of God. He starts His Ministry, leading the life of perfect love, and teaching the precepts of perfect love. He is endowed with supernatural power, and uses it for the works of love. But His miracles are a hindrance to His main purpose rather than a help, because they lead men to think of Him as a wonder-worker and excite in them a quite unspiritual interest and curiosity. So He commonly bids those whom He heals to be quiet about it; yet He still heals; for Love confronted with need must meet the need if it can.

The enquiry of John the Baptist is full of interest. He had once recognised the Lord for what He was. But he has begun to doubt because he hears what the Lord is doing. There are some blind folk who can see, some dumb folk who can speak, some deaf folk who can hear, even some dead folk raised to life and some devils vanquished; but where is the throwing down of strongholds and the uplifting of the meek, that should be the evidence of Messiah's presence in the world? So he sends to ask " Art thou he that should come or do we look for another? " The answer directs his attention to the causes of his doubt; let John consider it all again — with the addition " that the poor have the good news proclaimed to them; and blessed is he who is not scandalised at me " (*St. Matthew* xi, 1-6; *St. Luke* vii, 18-23). If we follow this advice what do we find? Power — yes, but the marvel is not in the power. What we find is power in complete subordination to love; and that is something like a definition of the Kingdom of God.

At first the Ministry was public. Then came a change, and the Lord began to concentrate attention on the Twelve whom He chose " that they might be with him " (*St. Mark* iii, 14). At about the same time He spoke the Parable of the Sower. To us it seems so beautiful in its simplicity that we are puzzled at the association with it of the dark words of Isaiah — about seeing and not perceiving (*St. Mark* iv, 11, 12). But we must ask what was the Word which this Sower had been scattering; it was not exhortation to virtue; it was the proclamation of the Kingdom of God. And it was very hard for men trained in the Jewish tradition to believe that the Kingdom of God is something scattered broadcast, which here meets with failure, there with brief success which gives place to failure, and only occasionally reaches full success. So in His explanation He says to the chosen few " Unto you is given the mystery — (the secret disclosed to initiates) — of the Kingdom of God, but unto those that are without all things are done in parables that seeing they may see and not perceive ", etc. (*St. Mark* iv, 10, 12).

But if the method of the Kingdom is to be that of Love winning answering love what the Parable of the Sower sets forth is inevitably true concerning it.

Having chosen the Twelve " that they might be with Him ", he takes them on two long journeys on foot, outside the areas of Jewish controversy, so that they may come to an intimate knowledge of Him. First they go to Tyre and Sidon, and, after return from there, to Caesarea Philippi; and now He feels that they are ready, and He asks whom men suppose Him to be. They mention the various guesses. Then — " Who say ye that I am? " — and Peter with a leap of inspired insight answers " Thou art the Messiah ". The Lord recognises that this is not something that He has been told, though John the Baptist long before had pointed to it; it is a revelation from heaven in answer to his loyalty.

Then the Lord, having been freely recognised, begins two new things: first a new teaching — " The Son of Man must suffer ". This is the new conception which takes the place of all those rejected at the outset in the wilderness; and St. Peter is not ready for it; but it is necessary. The Son of Man *must* suffer. For the manifestation of love, by which it wins its response, is always sacrifice. The principle of sacrifice is that we choose to do or to suffer what apart from our love we should not choose to do or to suffer. When love is returned this sacrifice is the most joyful thing in the world, and heaven is the life of joyful sacrifice. But in a selfish world it must be painful, and the pain is the source of triumph.

As He begins to give the new teaching, and now reiterates it frequently, so He starts at once on that journey, near the beginning of which He ascends the Mount of Transfiguration, and at the end of which He ascends the Hill of Calvary. In the ecstasy of the Transfiguration the theme of discourse between the Head of the Law, the Head of the Prophets and the Head of the New Order is the Exodus which He will accomplish at Jerusalem; the word Exodus carries a double meaning — for Him decease, for His people deliverance. On the journey to Jerusalem, as the Messiah marches on His capital, two disciples ask if they may be specially near Him in His glory. His answer is " Can you share my sacrifice? " — for the sacrifice *is* the glory. On reaching Jerusalem He challenges the High Priests by deliberately fulfilling Zechariah's prophecy in the Triumphal Entry. They must either accept Him or condemn Him to death for blasphemy, and He knows which they will do. He speaks repeatedly of His Coming as imminent; there is nothing said about a Second Coming, though there is truth in the expectation so expressed. But the Lord speaks only of the Coming of the Son of Man. Before the High Priest He declares that this is now a present fact. " From henceforth there shall be the Son of Man seated on the right hand of God and coming in the clouds of heaven " (*St. Luke* xxii, 69; cf. *St. Matthew* xxvi, 64). In each case the translation " hereafter " is a mere mistake. It is $\dot{\alpha}\pi$' $\ddot{\alpha}\rho\tau\iota$ in *St. Matthew* and $\dot{\alpha}\pi\grave{o}$ $\tau o\hat{v}$ $\nu\hat{v}\nu$ in *St. Luke*—the different expression for the same substance makes strong evidence). Daniel's prophecy, He claims, is then and there fulfilled.

In power the Kingdom was established when Christ was lifted up upon the Cross. From that moment it is true that " He cometh with clouds "; that is present fact. He reigns from the Tree. But not all have eyes to perceive; and the time when " every eye shall see Him " is still future, and this is the truth in the expectation of a Return or Second Coming.

The progress of the Kingdom consists in the uprising within the hearts of men of a love and trust which answer to the Love which shines from the Cross and is, for this world, the glory of God — the shining forth of His very self; and that newly experienced power of love and trust is the activity of the Holy Spirit, the Paraclete, who could not be given till Jesus was glorified (*St. John* vii, 39).

There remains a final consummation which involves a change in our mortal state and a removal of our present limitations. The Kingdom cannot come in all its perfection in this world for at least two reasons. First, it is a fellowship of all generations; secondly, every child that is born, being a nucleus of that Original Sin which is self-centredness, disturbs such degree of approximation as has been reached. Consequently here the figure of the Kingdom is the Cross, for in this world it is always winning its triumph by sacrifice; but the Cross is the symbol, not of failure but of triumph — a triumph to be made perfect in God's chosen time.

This is a purely Johannine picture of the Person and Work of Christ. My contention is that it is in fact the picture presented by the Synoptists, though they themselves had not fully grasped its meaning, which the Beloved Disciple first apprehended and declared.

As a confirmation of this view we may recall the fact that the " Sayings " of Christ recorded in the papyri discovered at Oxyrrynchus give us teaching which is strongly Johannine in substance without any of the distinctively Johannine phraseology. This evidence, the value of which is still a matter of some dispute, supports the view here taken, that the mind of Jesus Himself was what the Fourth Gospel disclosed, but that the disciples were at first unable to enter into this, partly because of its novelty, and partly because of the associations attaching to the terminology in which it was necessary that the Lord should express Himself. Let the Synoptists repeat for us as closely as they can the very words He spoke; but let St. John tune our ears to hear them.

NOTES

(a) *On the Following Translation*

I have set out from the Revised Version as Westcott would have wished it to be. No doubt he exaggerated the importance for Hellenistic Greek of some distinctions that are of great importance for classical Greek — e.g. between the aorist and the perfect tenses. But it was a good fault on the whole for an expositor. I have in a similar way sometimes gone to excess in retaining the order of the Greek words (for this sometimes suggests a valuable emphasis), and also in choosing words and phrases which exaggerate the shade of meaning conveyed by the original. For the purpose in view this is preferable to a better English which misses or obscures these *nuances*. But at all times my translation is intended for private reading with a view to personal meditation. It is not intended as a translation of the original into the most adequate English for reading aloud; for such a purpose it would be (so far as it is distinctive) a very bad translation. Its aim is to supply for those who cannot refer to the Greek original some of the additional illumination which is obtainable from that source. It is hoped that readers will have at hand a copy of the Revised Version in which references may be looked up.

(b) *On Dislocations of the Text*

I have a strong initial prejudice against any suggestion of dislocation in the text. But the arguments for supposing that Chapter VI should precede Chapter V, and that in Chapter VII verses 15-24 should be placed at the beginning of the chapter, are extremely strong. They are set out by Archbishop Bernard on pages xvi to xxx and following in the Introduction to his commentary. Here it is enough to say that the rearrangement proposed not only makes many particular phrases, and the narrative as a whole, far more easily intelligible, but has some objective support in the order followed by Tatian (*c.* 170 A.D.).

The other rearrangements proposed by Bernard seem to me far less probable; in particular, though the insertion of Chapters XV and XVI in the course of our Chapter XIII has some advantages, it also involves some disadvantages. In any case, the grounds for these rearrangements are remote from the purpose of these " readings "; as it is for the convenience of readers to follow the familiar arrangement unless there is very strong reason to vary it, I make no transpositions except in V, VI and VII; and I believe that this course is not only convenient but correct.

B

ACT III

THE LORD AMONG HIS DISCIPLES

CHAPTERS XIII and XIV

The Feet Washing (xiii, 1-20)

1-11. Now before the feast of the Passover Jesus, knowing that his hour was come that he should depart out of this world unto the Father, having loved his own, those in the world, to the utmost shewed his love to them. And during supper, the devil having already put it into the heart of Judas Iscariot, Simon's son, to betray him, knowing that the Father had given all things into his hands, and that he was come forth from God and went to God, he riseth from the supper and layeth aside his garments, and taking a towel girded himself; then he poureth water into the ewer, and began to wash the disciples' feet and to wipe them with the towel with which he was girded. So he cometh to Simon Peter. He saith to him, " Lord, dost *thou* wash *my* feet? " Jesus answered and said to him, " What *I* do *thou* knowest not now, but thou shalt understand here-after ". Peter saith to him, " Thou shalt by no means wash *my* feet to eternity ". Jesus answered him, " If I wash thee not, thou hast no part with me ". Simon Peter saith to him, " Lord, not my feet only but also my hands and my head ". Jesus saith to him, " He that is bathed needeth not save to wash his feet, but is clean in his whole person; and ye are clean, but not all ". For he knew the man that was betraying him, wherefore he said, " Ye are not all clean ".

Before the feast. So the Evangelist emphasises his chronology, which differs from that suggested by the Synoptists.

Knowing that his hour was come that he should depart out of this world unto the Father. The great moment which was still far off at Cana (ii, 4) is now near. The Lord knows this. Though His course is adjusted to the response of men or their lack of it, yet He moves through the drama as always master of circumstances, using each for the fulfilment of His own purpose, which now approaches its goal. That goal had always been that he should go unto the Father; for this means the attainment of the perfection of holiness and

love. He was " perfect " at every stage, as infant,
as boy, as youth, as man; but it is evident that there
is a height and depth of " perfection " in the man's
obedience to God which has no place in the boy's and
no meaning for the infant. " Perfect " at every stage,
He " yet learned obedience by the things which He
suffered, and having been made perfect (*or* full grown)
became to all them that obey Him the cause of eternal
salvation " (*Hebrews* v, 9).

His *hour*, then, *is come* that He should attain to
that perfection of holiness and love which is complete
union with the Father. Consequently what follows
is a manifestation of the meaning of that " hour ".
*Having loved his own, those in the world, to the utmost
shewed he his love to them.* Love grows by the acts
that express it; what the Lord now does is at once
the manifestation and attainment of perfect love: *to
the utmost* (not " to the end ") — the limit is now
reached; it is the *bosom of the Father* (i, 18) in which,
in a sense, the Son had always lain, yet to which now
He comes in the completion of His self-offering.

During supper — while it was going on, not " when
it was ended " (A.V.). There was a sense of special
solemnity about this supper, and this seems to have
led to a dispute about precedence (*St. Luke* xxii, 24).
St. Luke tells us that the Lord answered this partly
in words which He is recorded to have used when the
Sons of Zebedee had claimed pre-eminence (*St. Mark*
x, 42-44), but continuing — " Whether is greater, he
that sitteth at meat or he that serveth? is not he that
sitteth at meat? but I am in the midst of you as he
that serveth " (*St. Luke* xxii, 27). St. John tells us that
He not only spoke, but acted what He said. As a
rebuke to their worldly strivings, He, their *Lord and
Master* (14) shewed them what dignity is in the
Kingdom of God by rendering to them the most menial
service that could be asked of a slave.

The scene for the consummation is fully set and

the actors have their parts. The purpose of Judas is
formed. The Lord's supreme opportunity is come.

*Knowing that the Father had given all things into his
hands and that he was come from God and went to God.*
The occasion of His action was the dispute among
the disciples about precedence; but it had a deeper
motive. He is possessed by a special sense of divine
commission and authority. How does He express
that sense? Does He order a throne to be placed
that He may receive the homage of His subjects?
No — *he riseth from the supper and layeth aside his
garments, and taking a towel girded himself; then he
poureth water into the ewer,*[1] *and began to wash the
disciples' feet and to wipe them with the towel with
which he was girded.* So He will display Divine
Majesty.

We rather shrink from this revelation. We are
ready, perhaps, to be humble before God; but we
do not want Him to be humble in His dealings with
us. We should like Him, who has the right, to glory
in His goodness and greatness; then we, as we pass
from His presence, may be entitled to pride ourselves
on such achievements as distinguish us above other
men.

But the worship of Jesus Christ makes that impossible to justify. We worship the Infant in the
manger, for whom there was no room in the inn. We
worship one who meets our obeisance by rendering to
us menial service. So far as that worship is genuine
and complete, pride is eliminated; for He whom we
worship is humility itself incarnate.

The divine humility shews itself in rendering
service. He who is entitled to claim the service of
all His creatures chooses first to give His service to
them. " The Son of Man came not to receive service

[1] The "ewer" is the vessel used for pouring the water over the feet of
the guests on their arrival, not a vessel (bason) into which it fell from their
feet, or in which their feet might be placed.

but to give it " (*St. Mark* x, 45). But man's humility does not begin with the giving of service; it begins with the readiness to receive it. For there can be much pride and condescension in our giving of service. It is wholesome only when it is offered spontaneously on the impulse of real love; the conscientious offer of it is almost sure to " have the nature of sin " (Article XIII), as almost all virtue has of which the origin is in our own deliberate wills. For unless the will is perfectly cleansed, its natural or original sin — the sin inherent in it of acting from the self instead of God as centre — contaminates all its works. So man's humility shews itself first in the readiness to receive service from our fellow-men and supremely from God. To accept service from men is to acknowledge a measure of dependence on them. It is well for us to stand on our own feet; to go through life in parasitic dependence on others, contributing nothing, is contemptible; but those who are doing their share of the world's work should have no hesitation in receiving what the love or generosity or pity of others may offer. The desire " not to be beholden to anybody " is completely unchristian. Of course, it is equally true that to take all and offer nothing is even more opposed to the Christian spirit.

But it is the service of God which we must above all be ready to accept. We say in the most familiar of the Collects, " O God, forasmuch as without thee we are not able to please thee —— " Our first thought must never be, " What can I do for God? " The answer to that is, Nothing. The first thought must always be " What would God do for me? " The answer may be put in many ways; one is that He would cleanse me. When I recognise that, I am both admitting that I need to be cleansed, and acknowledging that I cannot cleanse myself. Moreover it is to each singly that the cleansing service is offered, according to his own stains.

So he cometh to Simon Peter. This individual
approach leads Him to offer the cleansing service to
that loyal, generous, impulsive Simon. His loyalty
and generosity rebel. It is not any vice, but the
very virtue in him, that is horrified by the Lord's
demeanour. *Lord, dost* thou *wash* my *feet?* The
relationship between them renders such an action
incredible. As Simon Peter emphasised the pronouns
to display this incompatibility of lordship and service,
so the Lord emphasises the pronouns as He points
out the incapacity (at present) of the Disciple to understand the Master's purpose.

What I *do* thou *knowest not now, but thou shalt
understand hereafter.* Simon Peter does not question
that; he only knows that what is proposed is intolerable and must always remain so: *Thou shalt by no
means wash* my *feet to eternity.* Whatever others may
allow, he at least will never permit this outrage — no,
not to eternity. (Ah, Peter, you have struck the right
note there; for it is unto eternity that your Lord
would cleanse you.) But none can have fellowship
with Jesus save those whom He Himself has washed.
If I wash thee not, thou hast no part with me. That
swings Peter over to demand more than was offered:
Lord, not my feet only but also my hands and my head.
It is loyalty that speaks, and generosity, but it is not
faith; for the one thing Peter cannot do is leave the
Lord alone to act as He pleases; the loyalty and the
generosity are infected with self-will. So his eager
utterance is met by a calm moderation that has the
effect of a mild rebuke. *He that is bathed needeth not
save to wash his feet, but is clean in his whole person;
and ye are clean.*

Guests usually bathed before starting to a feast;
but, walking to the appointed place in sandals, they
would gather dust on their feet, and there was need for
that washing of the feet to which the slaves of the
host would attend. So it is said that the disciples are

clean every whit. They are cleansed by their fellowship with their Lord and by His teaching: *already
ye are clean because of the word which I have spoken to
you* (xv, 3). But they are come to the feast, the Last
Supper or First Eucharist, and to the glorification of
the Son of Man. The last traces of stain must be
cleansed away from those who are already clean in
their whole persons. *Ye are clean, but not all.* Even
in that company of friends there was one who had
withstood the cleansing influence. He had heard
the word but was not clean because of it. And the
Lord knew.

Every disciple and every company of disciples
begin by wanting to give service. No doubt it is
wise that the Church should, as far as possible, provide
opportunities for this. But every disciple and every
company of disciples need to learn that their first
duty is to let Christ serve them. We are not now
thinking of those outside; the way to win them is
often to give them some job of work to do so that
they may feel that they are wanted and can help, as
the Lord began His saving of the Woman of Samaria
by saying, *Give me to drink* (iv, 8). Here we are
thinking of those who are committed to discipleship.
For them the first duty is to let the Lord cleanse them
by His word in their whole persons, and still to let
Him cleanse them day by day from stains that come
from life in the world; and at all times to leave the
Lord to do with them as He will, not demanding
either that He should not humble Himself for their
sakes or that He should do them some service that
might correspond to their devotion but would have
no usefulness for His purpose. He knows what is
best. It may not be good for me to be purified at
once from some temptation of which I am ashamed.
I must not clamour for that grace which it would
most gratify me to possess. My part is to accept with
wondering reverence whatever service He is pleased to

offer, even when service takes the form of judgement:
" It is the Lord; let Him do what seemeth Him
good " (*I Samuel* iii, 18).

It is exactly the failure of such trust, the absence
of such surrender, that may make us enemies and
traitors while we are still in the company of His
friends. We may go to Church and say our prayers
and read our Bibles; the cleansing Word flows over
us; but if our hearts are closed we are not cleansed.
And the Lord knows the man that is betraying Him,
perhaps before that man knows it himself. So of
every company of Christians He may be saying *Ye
are not all clean.* Let each of us ask tremblingly,
Lord, is it I?

*

12-20. So when he had washed their feet, and taken his garments,
and sat down again, he said to them, " Do ye understand what I
have done to you? Ye call me The Master and The Lord, and ye
say well, for I am. If then I washed your feet, the Master and
the Lord, ye also ought to wash one another's feet. For I gave
you an example that, as I did to you, ye also may do. Amen, Amen
I say to you, a slave is not greater than his Lord, nor an apostle
greater than he that sent him. If ye know these things, blessed are
ye if ye do them. Not concerning you all do I speak; *I* know
whom I chose; but that the scripture may be fulfilled, He that
eateth my bread lifted up his heel against me. From now I tell you
before it come to pass, in order that, when it is come to pass, ye may
believe that I am. Amen, Amen I say to you, he that receiveth
whomsoever I shall send receiveth me, and he that receiveth me
receiveth him that sent me."

The Lord does not leave His acted parable without
interpretation. Once He had set a child in the midst
of them as an illustration of greatness in the Kingdom
of Heaven (*St. Matthew* xviii, 1-4). This time He,
the undoubted Great One, has rendered the menial
service. He is the Master or Teacher among His
pupils; He is the Lord among His slaves: and this
is the way in which He disciplines them. Most

searching discipline, penetrating to the inward springs of conduct and of character as stripes could never do! But if we are pupils of such a Master, slaves of such a Lord, the consequence is clear. We must act to one another as He acts towards us. We recognise the truth of this; the task is to act upon it — and we shirk that task. We would gladly wash the feet of our Divine Lord; but He disconcertingly insists on washing ours, and bids us wash our neighbour's feet. This is an argument that appears elsewhere in the Johannine writings. " If God so loved us, we also ought to love one another " (*I John* iv, 11). What gives cogency to the argument is the revealed character of God. It is not cogent argument to say, " If A loves B, B ought to love C," unless A loves B and C equally. But the test of my love to God is the question whether I love my neighbour; for I know that God loves him as He loves me, and love of the loving God must shew itself in love of all whom God loves. " If a man say ' I love God ' and hateth his brother, he is a liar " (*I John* iv, 20).

A slave is not greater than his lord, nor an apostle greater than he that sent him. The word used is actually *apostle*; it means " one that is sent "; but the choice of it is not an accident. The Apostles are " set in the Church first " (*I Corinthians* xii. 28), and it is specially needful for them to remember that they are not greater than their Lord, who shewed His greatness by washing the disciples' feet.

Not concerning you all do I speak. In that little group of intimate friends one was false. Perhaps he did not know even now how false his own heart was; but the Lord knew, as He had known at the crisis marked by the discourse upon the Bread of Life (vi, 70). He knows the measure of our faith and loyalty better than we do. He may know that it is sound at the core even when our hearts condemn us (*I John* iii, 20). But He may know that it is worthless even when we think it sound. I *know whom I chose*, that is, *what kind of men I chose.* The first pronoun is emphatic. There is no doubt or obscurity in the Lord's understanding of His followers (ii, 24, 25). He, at any rate, knew what manner of men they were whom He chose. And one was this hard nature. The divine love must pit itself against that hardness; if it prevail, a great triumph is won; if it fail in the first impact, that opens the way to a still greater triumph. But love must make its uttermost appeal, as very soon now it will (26). The Lord knows that it must fail; and He knows the terrible strain that this failure and its consequences will put upon the loyalty of the other disciples; they *shall be scattered every man to his own and shall leave me alone* (xvi, 32). He does not hope that while the hour of darkness lasts they will be believing; but He tells them now what is coming so that when it is come and the hour is passed they may recollect that He foretold it. So they will see that all which had dismayed them fell within His plan, and faith in Him would revive: *I tell you before it come to pass, in order that, when it is come to pass, ye may believe that I AM.*

From that assurance would spring the confidence with which they would proclaim the Gospel. They will know that they are sent by the Divine Lord; they will be His ambassadors; to receive them will be to receive Him. *An apostle is not greater than he that sent him*; but he carries the dignity and honour of the King whom he represents. *He that receiveth whomsoever I shall send receiveth me.* Even more than this is true. For the Lord Himself is the first Apostle (*Hebrews* iii, 1), and to receive Him is to receive the Father. So the greatest of all miracles is accomplished; the gulf between man and God is bridged, not by man's achievement, but by God's humiliation, and as a result " our fellowship is with the Father and with His Son Jesus Christ " (*I John* i, 3).

THE DESIGNATION OF THE TRAITOR

21-30. When Jesus had said this he was troubled in spirit and bare witness and said, " Amen, Amen I say to you that one from among you shall betray me ". The disciples began to look upon one another in bewilderment concerning whom he spake. There was one of his disciples, whom Jesus loved, reclining in Jesus' bosom. Simon Peter therefore beckons to him to ask who it might be. He, leaning back as he was upon Jesus' breast, saith to him, " Lord, who is it? " So Jesus answers, " He it is for whom I shall dip the morsel and shall give it to him ". So having dipped the morsel, he taketh and giveth it to Judas, the son of Simon Iscariot. And after the morsel then entered into that man Satan. Jesus therefore saith to him, " What thou doest, do more quickly ". But none of them that sat at meat with him understood with what intent he said this to him. For some were supposing, because Judas had the money box, that Jesus was saying to him, " Buy those things of which we have need for the feast ", or that he should give something to the poor. So, having received the morsel, that one went out immediately; and it was night.

The thought that one of His chosen friends should betray Him disturbs that serenity of mind which was unruffled before the taunts and threats of Pharisees and High Priests. *He was troubled in spirit.* The hostilities of enemies cannot wound the soul as does the disloyalty of a friend — " mine own familiar friend whom I trusted, who eateth my bread, hath lifted up his heel against me " (*Psalm* xli, 9). To us He has said, *I have called you friends* (xv, 15), and our unfaithfulness is the unfaithfulness of friends; our disloyalty is as the sin of Judas; and the Lord knows our hearts: *One from among you shall betray me.*

The scene is intensely vivid. The company is at table reclining each on his left elbow at an oblique angle to the table, so that the right hand is free to take the food. The Lord is in a central position, and the place to His left would according to custom be regarded as the place of chief honour. We do not know who occupied it. Sometimes it is assumed that St. Peter was placed there as recognised leader of

the Apostolic fellowship.   But though his eager and
impulsive nature often made him the spokesman,
there is no evidence that he had any special status;
and if he was in this position, his beckoning to St.
John (24) is hard to visualise.   On the other hand,
Judas was treasurer, and would very naturally be in
this place at the table; if he were, it was easy for the
Lord to give him the choice morsel, and to speak to
him so that the others did not catch His meaning or,
perhaps, His words.   St. Matthew records an inter-
change — " Is it I ? "   " Thou hast said " — in which
the answer cannot have been generally heard.   We
assume then that Judas was occupying the place of
honour on the left of the Lord.

To the right was the Beloved Disciple, John the
son of Zebedee.   As he reclined on his left elbow, his
head would be opposite the Lord's bosom, and could
be spoken of as resting in that bosom, that is to say
in the folds of His garment.   A slight movement
would lead to his leaning against the Lord's breast,
looking up into His face (25).

The Beloved Disciple is the type of complete
discipleship.   As the Son is *in the bosom of the Father*
(i, 18) so the disciple is in the bosom of the Incarnate
Son.

The other disciples were reclining in a similar
position at the other places round the table.

Into that circle of apparently intimate friendship
fall the words, *Amen, Amen I say to you that one from
among you shall betray me.*   What wonder that they
*began to look upon one another in bewilderment concern-
ing whom he spake.*   So when the word that should
make us search our own consciences is spoken we
look round to see at whom the shaft was launched.
There are few more moving moments in Bach's
Passion according to St. Matthew than the moment
when, after the Chorus of Disciples — " Lord, is it
I? ", the Chorale follows and every soul present

confesses, " My sin it was which bound thee ".

Simon Peter is not content to be bewildered. He beckons to the Beloved Disciple to ask who is the traitor. *He, leaning back as he was upon Jesus' breast, saith to him, " Lord, who is it ? "* So Jesus answers, " *He it is for whom I shall dip the morsel, and shall give it to him* ". The question is asked and answered, but secretly, and only the Beloved Disciple understands what follows.

It was customary for a host to shew special honour or favour to one of his guests by dipping a choice morsel in the dish and handing this to him. The Lord shews that special honour and favour to the disciple whom He knows to be planning treachery. He makes a last appeal, and watches to see its effect. St. John, who alone shares the secret, watches also ; and what he saw he wrote : *after the morsel then entered into that man Satan.* The traitor's face went dark, and the Lord knew that the appeal had failed. In that moment of tense feeling His one desire is that what must come should come quickly. " How am I straitened till it be accomplished " (*Luke* xii, 50). *What thou doest, do more quickly.* The rest suppose that this is some command to hasten an ordinary duty or task. But Judas understands ; and St. John understands. So, *having received the morsel, that one went out immediately; and it was night.*

Judas moves to the door and opens it; St. John looks through it from the lighted room to the darkness outside. Judas goes of his own will from that light into that darkness, from the presence of the Light of the World into the outer darkness. There are no more pregnant words in the whole of literature than these — *and it was night.*

The Lord had known what was in Judas' mind. Judas had made his compact with the Chief Priests after the supper at which Mary had anointed the feet of the Lord and brought censure on himself by his

reproach of her (*St. Mark* xiv, 1-11). As a result of
this the directions to the two disciples who were to
prepare for this *kiddush* or fellowship meal were given
in a kind of cypher (*St. Mark* xiv, 13-16). Judas
must not hear the description of the place so that he
would be able to lead the Temple-guard to it and there
carry out the arrest in convenient secrecy. That sacred
time in the Upper Room must be kept free from
interruption. So all arrangements are made, including the clue which the two disciples are to follow —
the man bearing a pitcher of water. The two disciples
follow him in silence to the appointed place, where
later the Lord joins them with the rest of the
Twelve.

Knowing the traitor's intention, what shall He do?
Nothing could be easier than to speak a word to loyal
and impulsive Simon Peter and the others. We know
there were two swords in that room (*St. Luke* xxii, 38);
and apart from any such violence as that suggests,
Judas could have been left gagged and bound while
the Lord escaped. So He would have saved His
life; and so He would have lost His Kingdom. He
had come to inaugurate the Kingdom of God, who is
Love. His method was to live the life of perfect love
and die the death of perfect love. He will not now
fall back on any other method. So He makes one last
appeal to the false disciple's loyalty by singling him
out for special honour. The appeal fails. "*What
thou doest, do more quickly.*" Judas passes out under
the Lord's protecting silence.

In that moment the Lord condemned Himself to
death. He can still no doubt call for "more than
twelve legions of angels" (*St. Matthew* xxvi, 53).
But humanly speaking the Cross is now inevitable;
events will lead to it; His doom is sealed; and He
has sealed it.

*

C

THE GLORIFICATION OF THE SON OF MAN
(xiii, 31–xiv, 31)

In that moment the Lord did certain things. What He did is already familiar to St. John's readers. He took the bread, calling it His Body, and broke it and gave it. He took the cup, calling it His Blood of the New Covenant, and bade the disciples drink of it. For in that moment He was by His own act breaking His Body and pouring out His Blood. Not many hours later He was *lifted up from the earth* upon the Cross. The act of will that led to this — the essential act of self-sacrifice — was the choice of love's way in dealing with the traitor—" by which will we have been sanctified through the offering of the body of Jesus Christ once for all " (*Hebrews* x, 10).

From the time of His Ascension onwards His followers have met together to unite themselves with Him in His sacrifice by doing again what He did at this, the spiritual crisis of the ministry. They meet in His Name, and He is in the midst of them; they are members of His Body and He acts through them. Still by the hands of the priest He takes the Bread which He calls His Body, breaks it and gives it. But we are that Body — " very members incorporate " therein. In union with His perfect sacrifice, we offer to God " ourselves, our souls and bodies, to be a reasonable, holy and lively sacrifice " to Him. Still we drink the Cup, that His Blood, His Life given in sacrifice and triumphant over death, may be in us the spring of eternal life in fellowship with Him. Whether or not He commanded us to use this rite, as I believe that He did, yet its significance and power consists in the fact that we do in remembrance of Him what He did " in the same night in which He was betrayed ", offering ourselves in the power of His self-offering.

As in that moment the Lord did certain things recorded by the Synoptists and already familiar to all

Christians when the Fourth Gospel was written, so in that moment He said certain things which it remained for St. John to record.

31-35. When therefore he was gone out, Jesus saith, " Now was glorified the Son of Man and God was glorified in him. If God was glorified in him, God shall also glorify him in himself, and straightway shall he glorify him. Little children, yet a little while I am with you; ye shall seek me, and as I said to the Jews, ' Whither I go ye cannot come ', to you also I say it now. A new commandment I give to you, that ye love one another — as I loved you, that ye also love one another. By this shall all men recognise that ye are my disciples, if ye have love one to another."

When he was gone out. He went freely; the Lord did not *cast him out* (vi, 37; ix, 34); he went out freely into the night. He goes to fulfil his compact with the Lord's enemies and to effect the Lord's condemnation and death; his going leads to his own unending shame and to the Lord's glory. *Now was glorified the Son of Man.* We picture the Lord watching the door, through which the outer night has been seen for a moment, until it is closed behind the traitor. Then at once He speaks. That going of Judas to hasten his treachery is the moment of the glorification of the Son of Man. For this is the kind of Messiah that He is; " the Son of Man must suffer " (*St. Mark* viii, 31); that is the way in which He will inaugurate His Kingdom. God is Love; His glory is supremely what most displays His love; the Passion, to which by letting Judas go, the Lord has condemned Himself, is the very focus of the glory of the Son of Man — of man as God meant him to be, of the Messiah who came to restore the divine image in Him.

It is not only Messiah's glory, but *God is glorified in Him.* The martyr wins for himself the crown of glory; but also by his death he gives glory to God. So in higher degree the Son of Man wins glory by His obedience unto death (*Philippians* ii, 8-11), but therein also gives glory to God whose love was supremely shewn by giving Him for the saving of the world (iii, 16). The Son of Man enters His own glory in the act of self-devotion; but thereby also He gives glory to God to whom He is devoted; and when we confess Him as Lord, we do this " to the glory of God the Father " (*Philippians* ii, 11).

But if so, *if God was glorified in Him* in that devoted act of choice which let the traitor go, God will not leave it there. God will vindicate that self-devotion in the perfected union of the Son with Himself, towards which the words recorded in xvii, 5 are the aspiration and of which the Ascension is the proclamation; *God shall also glorify him in himself.* Nor is this a far-off consummation; it is now at hand; *and straightway shall he glorify him.*

The Lord has spoken of what the great moment — for ever commemorated in the breaking of the Bread and the pouring of the Wine — means for Himself. He goes on to speak of what it means for His friends. It means that there can only be a brief continuance of the form of intercourse that they have known; *yet a little while I am with you.* There is an aspect of the coming separation of which He will speak later (xvi, 7). But separation there will be. He is going where they cannot follow. They will seek Him; it is not said, as it was to the Jews, that they will not find him (vii, 34), but it is said now to them as it was said earlier to the Jews — *whither I go ye cannot come.*

As we have seen, this phrase does not mean only that the Lord is to die so that those who still live on earth cannot accompany Him; it stands for that union with the Father which has been His without defect from the beginning, but is His in all its plenitude in and through the Passion (*Hebrews* ii, 10; v, 8, 9). That is a goal to which even the disciples cannot attain until a new power is come upon them, though then it will be possible (36).

This unattainable goal is that perfection of love which Christ Himself has shewn. This *new commandment*, to love as Christ has loved, is the impossible thing, except so far as we are " in Christ " (to use St. Paul's great phrase) as the branches are in the Vine (xv, 5, 10, 12). He Himself will make it possible for us, but till then it is not possible.

Does this command supersede the Second Great Commandment " Thou shalt love thy neighbour as thyself "? No — that stands as the general rule of our relation to all men, with the understanding of the word " neighbour " which it receives from the Parable of the Good Samaritan; my " neighbour " is anyone with whom I have anything at all to do, even by accident, and even though he is the kind of person that I naturally hate or despise. I am to care as much for his interest and welfare as for my own; and I need a most penetrating " conversion " before I do that. But here the Lord speaks, not of our relation to mankind generally, but of the special bond of love that should unite all fellow-Christians. Within the Christian fellowship each is to be linked to each by a love like that of Christ for each. That is the new commandment; and obedience to it is to be the evidence to the world of true discipleship. If the Church really were like that, if every communicant had for every other a love like that of Christ for him, the power of its witness would be irresistible, and out of that nucleus of self-giving love — love like that of Christ upon the Cross — would flow the power making men generally love their neighbours as themselves. The Old Commandment stands as a universal, and universally neglected, requirement; the New Commandment *that ye love one another as I loved you* has a narrower range and an intenser quality. When the Church keeps the New Commandment, the world may keep the Old.

*

36–xiv, 3. Simon Peter saith to him, " Lord, whither goest thou? "
Jesus answered, " Whither I go thou canst not follow me now,
but thou shalt follow me afterwards ". Peter saith to him, " Lord,
why cannot I follow thee now? My life for thee I will lay down."
Jesus answered, " Thy life for me wilt thou lay down? Amen,
Amen I say to thee, the cock shall by no means crow till thou hast
denied me thrice. Let not your hearts be troubled; believe in
God, and believe in me. In my Father's house are many resting-
places. If it were not so, should I have told you that I go to prepare
a place for you? And if I go and prepare a place for you, I come
again and will receive you to myself, that where I am ye also
may be."

St. Peter is puzzled by this language about a
journey. To what place does it lead? The answer
had been given earlier (vii, 33), but there is reason to
think that Peter was not then present (see p. 176).
It will be given repeatedly later (xiv, 12, 28; xvi,
5, 10, 28). But the answer must gain its meaning
as the discourse proceeds; for it is a spiritual journey
on which the Lord is going. He goes to the Father.
This involves His death; and His death is involved,
not as a physical transition but as a spiritual sacrifice.
Therefore, instead of describing His destination, He
first insists on the incapacity of Peter and the rest to
follow now. They could die; but if they did, that
would not bring them where He is going; it would
not bring them to perfectly fulfilled union with the
Infinite Love. *Whither I go thou canst not follow me
now*. But later that will have become possible —
thou shalt follow me afterwards (cf. xxi, 19).

Still Peter cannot understand. He believes that
his loyalty is complete; he is ready to lay down life
itself for his Lord. *Why cannot I follow thee now?
My life for thee I will lay down*. It was no idle boast.
A few hours later Peter began to fight when fighting
meant certain death. So the Lord does not deny his
readiness to die. But He knows that another sort of
trial is coming, when the cause of the Lord will seem
to be lost, and Peter in utter depression, very cold,

will have to face mockery and jeers. Then he will fail. *Thy life for me wilt thou lay down? Amen, Amen I say to thee, the cock shall by no means crow till thou hast denied me thrice.*

We can imagine a little of the shock which those words gave to the hearers. To Peter himself it was such that through all the following scene, though others spoke, he, the readiest of all to speak, was silent. His next appearance is at xviii, 10, where he draws his sword and begins to fight for his Master, and would undoubtedly have then laid down his life if the Lord had not stopped the fighting. But great as was the shock to him, it was little less for his companions, and it is to all of them that the following words are addressed: *Let not your hearts be troubled; believe in God, and believe in me.* They were going to fail, and to fail badly. Peter would deny him; and of all it is written that they forsook him and fled (*St. Mark* xiv, 50). The failure must not become a cause of despair or dismay; rather let it teach its lesson. When we fail in our discipleship it is always for one of two reasons; either we are not trying to be loyal, or else we are trying in our own strength and find that it is not enough. The former is known to be sinful, but occasions no bewilderment. If we do not try, our lack of success is explained, though our failure to try may well fill us with dismay. The root of that failure, however, is the feebleness of our faith as a settled direction of mind and will. If our habitual faith were stronger we should always try to be loyal. When we try in our own strength and find it insufficient, this too is evidence of defect in faith. Our faith is strong enough to prompt us to try; but it is not strong enough to claim the power of God for His service. Until our trust is perfect, we need to supplement our habitual reliance upon God with special acts of trust — probably expressed in secret but conscious prayer — at moments of acute difficulty or temptation.

Failure, then, always proves that faith is insufficient. It should drive us back upon God, forgetfulness of whose grace has caused the failure. Then every fall into sin can become the occasion for growth in grace. *Let not your hearts be troubled; trust God, and trust me.*

One who so faces his own failures is steadily advancing on the pilgrim's way; he, like his Master, is going *to the Father.* More than this; if he is thus travelling the right way at all, he is at home with the Father all the time. *In my Father's house are many resting-places. If it were not so, should I have told you that I go to prepare a place for you? And if I go and prepare a place for you, I come again and will receive you to myself.*

The *resting-places* (μοναί) are wayside caravanserais — shelters at stages along the road where travellers may rest on their journey. It was the custom in the East — and still is, where railways and motor cars have not yet penetrated — for travellers to send a dragoman forward to make preparation in the next of those resting-places along the road, so that when they came they might find in it comfort as well as shelter. Here the Lord presents Himself as our spiritual dragoman, who treads the way of faith before us — the " captain and perfecter of faith," τὸν τῆς πίστεως ἀρχηγὸν καὶ τελειωτήν (*Hebrews* xii, 2) — and makes ready to welcome us. It may be that we are still far from perfect fellowship with the Father; like Peter, we are about to deny our Lord, or like the rest, we are about to forsake him in flight. We have a long journey of many days before us ere our pilgrimage is accomplished. But there are, by God's mercy, *many resting-places.* Otherwise of what avail would be the promise of the Lord to *prepare a place* for us? If it were only in the realm of ultimate attainment, would He mock us with the promise of a welcome there? *Should I have told you that I go to prepare a place for you?*

There has not been recorded any promise in those precise terms. But the whole tenor of His teaching has been such as to imply the companionship of His disciples with Him as He goes to the Father. This is not the only instance of reference to former sayings which are not precisely recorded (cf. vi, 36; xi, 40). Apart from this, the construction of the words which has been adopted is preferable to the others which are grammatically possible, and it is therefore adopted here.

The Lord calls us to absolute perfection; but He points us here and now to what is for each one the next stage, the next *resting-place*, on the way to it. And as we follow, we find Him there to welcome us. More than that — He comes to lead us there. *If I go and prepare a place for you, I come again and will receive you to myself.* The image of dragoman and caravanserai is still employed. There is no special reference to a final Parousia or Return in Glory, though that thought is in place in reference to the final stage. Our spiritual dragoman, who has gone forward to make preparation, returns to encourage us and lead us to the resting-place prepared. That resting-place is fellowship, fuller than before, with the Lord — *that where I am ye also may be* — until the last stage is reached, towards which we press on, " the goal of the call upward which God gives in Christ Jesus " (*Philippians* iii, 14).

Every Christian must know something of what is here described. We reach a certain stage of fellowship with Christ, in spiritual apprehension and moral attainment, and find great joy in it. But this seems to fade, until we become conscious that we are called to something higher. The Lord is gone before us to prepare the next resting-place. Then everything depends upon our response. We may stay where we are, becoming more and more torpid in spirit. Or we may, in St. Paul's phrase, " press on ". If we do

this, we find the Lord meeting us and leading us to
the next resting-place. Our sense of fellowship with
Him revives, and with this our joy in it. Then the
process is repeated. So we make progress, "from
glory to glory" (*II Corinthians* iii, 18) till we are
"transformed into the same image". The new "call
upwards" is sometimes an awareness of something
positively wrong, a "weight" that must be laid
aside (*Hebrews* xii, 1), and sometimes an apprehension
of service to be rendered which calls for completer
self-devotion. If we refuse to start on the new stage
of our journey we forfeit the companionship of the
Lord; but so soon as we even start, He is at our side
again, returning that He may receive us to Himself.

. . . *If I go* . . . *I come again.* These do not
merely follow upon one another. His "going" is
itself a "coming". For He goes to the Father, to
whom all things are present, so that by His departure
He becomes more accessible than ever before: see
xx, 17 and comment there.

In this wonderful passage there is another thought,
the most wonderful of all. These *many resting-places*,
marking the stages of our spiritual growth, are in the
Father's house. If we are travelling heavenwards, we
are already in heaven. And though the perfection
of communion with the Father to which the Lord is
gone is a place where we cannot follow him now, it is
none the less true, not only that we shall follow Him
afterwards, but that even now, if our faces are set the
right way " our fellowship is with the Father and with
His Son Jesus Christ " (*I John* i, 3).

Let us hear the amazing words again — we,
who are His disciples and would like to think that
we could lay down our lives for Him, but also fear
lest this night we may deny Him: *Let not your hearts
be troubled; trust God; and trust Me. In my Father's
house are many resting-places. If it were not so, should
I have told you that I go to prepare a place for you?*

And if I go and prepare a place for you, I come again and will receive you to myself, that where I am, ye also may be.

"'Yea: I come quickly.' Amen: come, Lord Jesus" (*Revelation* xxii, 20).

*

Our Access to the Father

4-11. "And whither I go, ye know the way." Thomas saith to him, "Lord, we know not whither thou goest; how know we the way?" Jesus saith to him, "I am the way, and the truth, and the Life. No one cometh to the Father except through me. If ye had recognised me, ye would know my Father also. From now ye are recognising Him and have seen Him." Philip saith to him, "Lord, shew us the Father, and it sufficeth us". Jesus saith to him, "So long a time have I been with you and hast thou not recognised me, Philip? He that hath seen me hath seen the Father. How dost *thou* say, 'Shew us the Father'? Dost thou not believe that I am in the Father, and the Father in me? The words that I say to you I speak not from myself, but the Father who abideth in me doeth his works. Believe me that I am in the Father and the Father in me; or else on account of the works themselves believe me."

The goal of our journey is unknown except in its formal description. It is Heaven; it is perfect fellowship with the Father; but what those phrases really mean it is beyond our faculties to grasp: "Things which eye saw not and ear heard not, and which entered not into the heart of man, whatsoever things God prepared for them that love him" (*I Corinthians* ii, 9). But though the goal is thus unknown and unknowable to us, yet the Lord declares that we know the way.

To Thomas, loyal and literal-minded Thomas, this is bewildering. We choose our road with reference to our destination. We do not go to a railway station and ask the officials to recommend a direction and a train; it is only because we know where we mean to go that we can reasonably even ask for advice how to start. *" Whither I go, ye know the way."* *" We know not whither thou goest, how know we the way? "* *" I am the way."* Though the goal is unknown, the way is well known, for it is the Lord Himself. We have to pass through Him if we are to come to the Father; we must be so united with Him that as He offers Himself to the Father He offers us also. *No one cometh to the Father except through me.*

We are to pass " through the veil, that is to say, His flesh " (*Hebrews* x, 20). The human nature of Christ conceals the Deity from us, as it did from the Jews, until we are united with it and find the Deity indwelling it. We must *eat the flesh of the Son of Man and drink his blood* (vi, 53) so that His humanity becomes the substance of our very being; then we find that " our fellowship is with the Father " (*I John* i, 3).

Only because He is more than an individual man can He be *the way* for us. Shakespeare is not himself " the way " for me to write poetry, nor is even St. Francis " the way " for me to be a Christian. These shew me how poetry can be written and how Christianity can be lived; they have a way of doing it, but neither of them is a way by which others may do it. But Jesus is not only a man who trod the way to God: He is Himself that supreme Spirit " in whom we live, and move, and have our being " (*Acts* xvii, 28). We can become " very members incorporate " in His Body as we cannot in the body of any other. We come to the Father *through* Him, and He is *the way.*

The thought which has been expressed by reference to His Deity coupled with the Divine Omnipresence is, in the text, brought forward in another way. *I am the way, and the truth, and the Life.* It is possible for the Lord to be Himself *the way* because He is also *the truth and the Life.* He is *the truth.* Truth is the perfect correlation of mind and reality; and this is actualised in the Lord's Person. If the Gospel is true and God is, as the Bible declares, a Living God, the

ultimate truth is not a system of propositions grasped
by a perfect intelligence, but is a Personal Being apprehended in the only way in which persons are ever fully
apprehended, that is, by love.   The Incarnation is not
a condescension to our infirmities, so that " Truth
embodied in a tale " may enter in at the " lowly door "
of human minds.   It is the only way in which divine
truth can be expressed, not because of our infirmity
but because of its own nature.   What is personal can
be expressed only in a person.

This personal truth is also *the Life*, the vitalising
energy of all that lives.   Already, even while we
recognise Him not, He is the well-spring of what
vitality we have.   Our task is not laboriously to follow
Him, nor in some way to transform our nature; our
task is to recognise what is already and always fact,
that all progress we make is through Him, all knowledge we gain is of Him, all energy we exercise is from
Him.   *He is the way and the truth and the Life.*

" *Ye know the way.*"   " *I am the way.*"   It starts
where each one stands.   We do not have to find its
starting-place.   It starts here where we are.   For
there is no conceivable combination of circumstances
in which it is not possible to shew love; and " God
is love; and he that abideth in love, abideth in
God, and God abideth in him " (*I John* iv, 16).

So close is the union of Christ with the Father
that if we know Him for what He is we are thereby
brought to knowledge of the Father: *If ye had
recognised me, ye would know my Father also.*   The disciples are beginning truly to know their Lord, so that
they may even be said, in and through that knowledge, to have seen the Father ; *From now ye are
recognising him and have seen him.*   Apart from this
understanding of Christ there is no vision of God (i, 18);
but through this the vision of God is actual experience.   Yet the disciples do not yet grasp the meaning
of their fellowship with Christ ; they do not appreciate

their unique privilege, in that they saw and heard the things which many prophets and kings desired to see and hear, yet saw and heard them not (*St. Luke* x, 24). So Philip, half-consciously perceiving that they stand on the brink of a great fulfilment, utters the deepest yearning of the human heart: " *Lord, shew us the Father, and it sufficeth us* ". That is the craving which alone causes all our restlessness; if that be sated, all desire is quiet. It is much to learn that this is our one great need. " Like as the hart desireth the water-brooks, so longeth my soul after thee, O God. My soul is athirst for God, yea, even for the living God: when shall I come to appear before the presence of God?" (*Psalm* xlii, 1, 2). " Whom have I in heaven but thee; and there is none upon earth that I desire in comparison of thee. My flesh and my heart faileth: but God is the strength of my heart and my portion for ever" (*Psalm* lxxiii, 25, 26). " When I wake up after thy likeness, I shall be satisfied with it " (*Psalm* xvii, 15).

But Philip's request is for something more than a manifestation of God as even devout Jews thought of Him. What was novel in the religious language of the Lord was His constant, His almost invariable, use of the word " Father " as the name of God. It is as though Philip said, " We have long believed in God, but make Him plainly known to us as Father and we shall be satisfied: *Shew us the Father, and it sufficeth us* ".

It is the utterance of the common need of all mankind. But the Christian has no right to make it. For him the satisfaction of that need is already available. Has our discipleship yet taught us that Jesus Himself is the satisfaction of all that hunger expressed, for example, by the Psalmists in the verses which we have quoted? If not, we have not learnt our lesson and our discipleship is incomplete. " *So long time have I been with you and hast* thou *not recognised me, Philip?*" He had been in their company (the word *you* is plural) and here is one of that company who still does not recognise Him for what He is. So too He is in His Body the Church, and here is myself, a member of that Body, who have little more than an intellectual recognition of Him; my heart does not in fact find yet that constant joy in His presence, that " peace which passeth understanding ", which must be the result of communion with the Eternal God. I am assured, with no tremor of doubt, that fellowship with Jesus is fellowship with God; since, then, it has not the effect of fellowship with God, it must be an imperfect fellowship. I have no power to make it perfect; but when I desire that it should be perfect, I can expose myself to the influence which can make it so, and which streams from the Person of Jesus, the Word Incarnate. " Lord, I believe, help thou mine unbelief." Lord, I love; help thou my lack of love. *Shew us the Father, and it sufficeth us.*

" *He that hath seen me, hath seen the Father.*" Those are the words that we long to hear. We cannot fully grasp that supreme truth, as we should if our discipleship were perfect. We need to hear them over and over again, to let the sound of them constantly play upon our ears, the meaning of them perpetually occupy our minds, the call in them unceasingly move our wills. Jesus our Lord is " the image of the invisible God " (*Colossians* i, 15), " the effulgence of his glory and the very image of his substance " (*Hebrews* i, 3). In adoration, in supplication, in dedication, let us take care always to address ourselves to God as He is seen in Jesus Christ. Never ask in prayer for any blessing till you are sure your mind is turned to Jesus Christ; then speak to God as you see Him there. " This is the true God and eternal life. Little children guard yourselves from idols " (*I John* v, 20, 21).

How are we to hold our minds to this truth ? It must be by appreciation of that quality in the Lord which in this Gospel is most frequently emphasised,

His constant dependence for all He is and does and says upon the Father. Can we behold that glory which is not His own but streams through Him from the Father (i, 14)? *Dost thou not believe that I am in the Father and the Father in me? The words that I say to you I speak not from myself, but the Father who abideth in me doeth his works.* The *words* of Christ are *works* of God. No man can do God's work; only God can do that. But God can indwell a man and work through him; and this general principle was supremely illustrated by Him in whom Manhood was taken into God.

So there are two levels of faith possible to us. Best of all is that intuitive faith which apprehends Deity when face to face with it and can accept the claim which its very nature must make. *Believe me that I am in the Father and the Father in me.* But if that is beyond us, then it is still possible for us to face the works which He does and, recognising them as divine, acknowledge that He who does them must Himself be God: *or else on account of the works themselves believe me.*

*

THE EFFECTS OF FAITH

12-14. "Amen, Amen, I say to you, He that believeth on me, the works that I do shall he do also, and greater than these shall he do, because I go to the Father. And whatsoever ye shall ask in my name, this will I do, that the Father may be glorified in the Son. If ye shall ask anything in my name, I will do it."

The *works* are signs and evidences of the Deity of Christ. But in the days when He was " straitened " (*St. Luke* xii, 50) they could not be convincing to any except those specially qualified by purity of heart to see God at work. Even the Baptist had been disappointed rather than impressed by them (*St. Matthew* xi, 2). There would be more persuasive evidence when, having accomplished His journey *to the Father,*

He empowered His disciples, united with one another in Him as His Body, to act as His representatives in the world. The *greater works* need not be more startling miracles, for the degree of our amazement may be due to the scantiness of our knowledge or the vulgarity of our taste as truly as to the intrinsic marvel of what is accomplished. St. Paul found his converts disposed to give special honour to " speaking with tongues " as a peculiar manifestation of the Spirit, and had to insist on the superiority of " charity " as a " more excellent way " (*I Corinthians* xii and xiii). That a respectable citizen should love his neighbour as himself is less likely to be announced in double-column headlines than his utterance of ecstatic gibberish in a public place; but it would be quite as unusual, and a far surer sign of the divine presence and activity in him.

In scale, if not in quality, the *works* of Christ wrought through His disciples are greater than those wrought by Him in His earthly ministry. It is a greater thing to have founded hospitals all over Europe and in many parts of Asia and Africa than to have healed some scores or some hundreds of sick folk in Palestine; and it is to the Spirit of Christ at work in the hearts of men that we owe the establishment of hospitals. The accomplishment of the journey *to the Father* means, among other things, that the Lord is no longer " straitened " by the limitations of our mortal state; He is where God is, and that is everywhere. His *works* are no longer limited to Palestine but are diffused over the world. The transformation of Uganda is one of them; the inspiring record of the Universities' Mission to Central Africa is another; the fellowship of Chinese and Japanese Christians while their nations are at war is a third. The power to do these *greater works* through the agency of His disciples is His because He is gone *to the Father*.

D

Indeed there is no limit to what He may do through us, or (which is the same thing) to what we may do in His Name. To act in the name of another is to act as His representative. When we pray in the Name of Christ, we pray as His representatives; in other words, we are then praying for what is already His will, but for a part of that will which He waits to fulfil until we recognise Him as the source of blessing by asking it of Him; then immediately His power is released and becomes effective; *whatsoever ye shall ask in my name, this will I do.* But there is a motive behind this. It is not a merely mechanical release of power. There is something more at work than a law of cause and effect; the bestowal of blessing, when that condition is fulfilled on which depends its actual benefit, is for the glory of the Father. This is the supreme motive of every activity of the Son and the supreme object which every created thing exists to promote; our success, or health, or welfare is of very small importance in itself; only because God loves us, unlovely as we are, have we value in ourselves; that value is our value to Him; and what gives importance to our well-being is that it brings glory to God. This is not to say that the Son does not act for love of men; for God is love, and the glory of God is the shining forth and the victory of love. Yet it makes a vast difference whether we suppose that God loves us because we are lovable, or that He loves us, in spite of much in us which deserves His antagonism, because He is overflowing love. So the motive of the Son in granting these prayers which are in His Name or in accordance with His will must be *that the Father may be glorified* in the Son.

Yet this is not to be the last thought on the matter. The last thought, leading us forward to what follows, is the absolute assurance that prayers offered in the Name of Christ will be granted. *If ye shall ask anything in my name, I will do it.*

We can hope to rest in His Name only if and so far as there is complete union of our hearts and wills with His; and that union is love.

*

The Promise of the Comforter

15-26. "If ye love me, the commandments that are mine ye will observe. And I will ask the Father and he will send you, besides, a Comforter that he may be with you to eternity, the spirit of truth, whom the world cannot receive, because it observeth him not neither recogniseth him; but *ye* are recognising him because he abideth with you and shall be in you. I will not leave you bereft; I am coming to you. Yet a little while and the world taketh note of me no more, but ye take note of me, that I live and ye shall live. In that day ye will recognise that I am in my father and ye in me and I in you. He that hath my commandments and observeth them, he it is that loveth me; and he that loveth me shall be loved by my Father, and I will love him and manifest myself to him."

There saith to him Judas, not Iscariot, "Lord, what then has happened that thou art about to manifest thyself to us and not to the world?" Jesus answered and said to him, "If any man love me, my word he will observe, and my Father will love him, and we shall come to him and make a resting-place with him. He that loveth me not doth not observe my words; and the word which ye hear is not mine, but the Father's who sent me. These things have I spoken to you while abiding with you; but the Comforter, the Spirit, the Holy One, whom the Father will send in my name, he will teach you all things and will bring to your remembrance all things which I said to you."

The whole of this passage, though long and packed with truths, must be considered together. First, love and obedience are coupled together, and both are associated with the coming of the Comforter (15, 16); then the meaning of that coming is partially disclosed (17-24); then the source of the Comforter's power in the historical ministry of Christ is made clear, and the thought of His coming is thus again linked with the love and obedience of disciples to their Lord (25, 26).

If ye love me, the commandments that are mine ye

will observe. This is a cumbrous translation, but there is a special emphasis on the word *mine*, and there is a special suggestion on the word *observe*. It is, as in viii, 51, the word which means " watch " rather than " fulfil ". The suggestion is that of a standard of reference and judgement rather than of a literal obedience to precepts. The commandments that are Christ's are such as do not lend themselves to detailed and exact fulfilment, for they concern the quality of spiritual life and not defined actions. We are to " believe on " Him; we are to love our neighbours as ourselves, and our fellow-Christians as Christ loved us. These cannot be obeyed with the same precision as commands to go to Church or to give a tenth of income for Church work. The commands of Christ will nearly always carry these and similar actions as incidental consequences of the obedience claimed, but they go beyond anything of this kind.

Having thus drawn out the special tone of the words chosen, we can return to the more familiar version. *If ye love me, ye will keep my commandments;* and if we don't, we shan't. Let no one deceive himself about that. There is no possibility of meeting His claim upon us, unless we truly love Him. So devotion is prior to obedience itself. I *cannot* obey unless I love; and if I am to love, I must be with Him whom I desire to love. Personal companionship with Christ is the first requirement, as it was for the disciples in Palestine. If we love Christ, and in whatsoever degree we love Christ, obedience will follow — not the external obedience of the slave who does what he is told, but the gladly given obedience of the friend or the son (xv, 15; *Romans* viii, 15) whose desire is to give pleasure.

Our love is cold. It is there, but it is feeble. It does not carry us to real obedience. Is there anything that I can do? No; there never is, except to hold myself in His presence; the initiative remains

with God.   But the Lord, who knows both the reality
and the poverty of our love, will supply our need.
I will ask the Father and he will send you, besides, a
Comforter that he may be with you to eternity.

The sending of the Comforter is due to the Son's
request.   Here as always He is the mediator between
the Father and men.   His love for His disciples,
which is itself the manifestation of the Father's love
for the world (iii, 16; v, 19), becomes the impulse of
the Father's action.   But the manifestation of divine
love in the Son had to come first (vii, 39) because this
is what calls forth the new response from our hearts,
or (to put it from the other side) breaks through the
hard shell of selfishness and self-complacency so that
the Comforter may enter.

The familiar translation *another Comforter*, though
literal, is misleading.   It implies that the Holy Spirit
is what Christ had been; and while this is true and
important and is implied in 18, it is not implied
here.   We find the same idiom in *St. Luke* xxiii, 32,
though the actual word used is different; the literal
translation there is, " And there were led also two
other malefactors with him to be put to death ".   The
English way of saying this is, " two malefactors as
well " or " besides ".   The point here is that the
Comforter comes, as the Son came, by mission from
the Father.   As the Father sent the Son (a truth perpetually reiterated) so also He will, at the Son's request,
send the Comforter.

The Comforter: it seems best to keep the familiar
phrase.   The only alternative is to transliterate and
say " the Paraclete ".   But this is not an English
word, and when it occurs in hymns strikes many as
exotic.   No translation will do it full justice;   the
Latinisation—Advocate, has to gain its meaning from
the actual use of it in this Gospel as much as Paraclete.
It represents one who is called in to stand by —
it may be as a witness, or as an adviser, or as an

advocate in the legal sense. The word "Comforter" was used by Wyclif and has remained in subsequent versions. Wyclif certainly understood it as meaning "strengthener" (*confortator*) rather than "consoler"; the suggestion is of one who makes us brave and strong by being brave and strong beside us. But to strengthen is the best of all ways to console, for it brings a bracing consolation and not a relaxing sympathy.

That He may be with you for ever. Already begins the preparation of the disciples for the separation which is at hand. Their Lord must *go away* (xvi, 7). It is true that He goes *to the Father* (28) and therefore is for ever available for them (*St. Matthew* xxviii, 20). But the old form of intercourse, so familiar and so dear, will have come to an end. There will be no such interruption in the abiding with them of the Comforter.

The Spirit of truth — the Spirit who is Himself the essence of truth and therefore also the Spirit who imparts or produces truth. The phrase carries both these meanings, and each is in itself a double meaning because of the subjective and objective aspects of truth. Truth, when we speak of knowing it, is the objective reality as it actually is, undistorted and completely apprehended; truth as a quality of the mind is sincerity, which includes positively the desire to apprehend reality completely and accurately, and negatively the absence of conflicting interests which may bias or blur the judgement. The Comforter is the source of both kinds of truth.

This title of the divine Spirit is sometimes specially valued by those who have not accepted the Gospel of the unique manifestation of God in Christ. They wish to follow, perhaps to worship, the *Spirit of truth* without first seeing God in Jesus Christ. They are right to pay all possible reverence to *the Spirit of truth* and some Christians can learn from them in this respect. When controversy arises, some theologians seem more concerned to ask concerning any proposition " Is it orthodox? " than to ask " Is it true? " Such need the reminder of Coleridge: " He, who begins by loving Christianity better than truth, will proceed by loving his own sect or church better than Christianity, and end in loving himself better than all ".[1]

Yet those who follow truth without finding it incarnate in the historical Jesus of Nazareth, cannot claim to be led by that Spirit to whom reference is here made. He is one whom *the world cannot receive, for it observeth him not neither recognises him.* The world — that is, the natural order apart from God — pays no attention to the Spirit, and when it sees Him at work cannot recognise what is happening. It must first have the eyes of the mind opened by the touch of Christ. Certainly many who are not professing Christians are more sensitive to the Spirit of truth than many who are; but that profession is not here in question. *The world* is contrasted with those who have both been companions of Christ and have become His disciples, in whom response to the revelation and consequently the power of the Spirit are already discernible: *ye are recognising him, because he abideth with you and shall be in you.* The disciples already have some awareness of the Spirit, who is supremely known as a response to the love of God manifested in Christ, because as a company they have been taking note of His glory (ii, 11), though this has not yet shone forth in its fulness, and till that has happened the Spirit will not be active in all His power (vii, 39). At present it is rather in the apostolic company than in the individual disciples severally that the power is at work — *he abideth with you.* He will later indwell each one — *he shall be in you.* That is the necessary order. We are brought to Christ and received by Him into the fellowship of His Church; in that company we find the Spirit at work; as we are

[1] *Aids to Reflection : Moral and Religious Aphorisms,* xxv.

shaped and moulded by His influence thus diffused and exercised, we begin to find it within ourselves; this individual experience of the Spirit is normally subsequent to, and consequent upon, our experience of His activity in the Church or Christian fellowship. The two stages are marked ritually by Baptism and Confirmation.

This coming of the Spirit is in a sense a coming of Christ Himself; so the Lord can pass in His teaching from one to the other. For St. John, as we shall see more clearly later, the Day of the Lord's Resurrection is the Day of the Advent of the Spirit. It is not true that the Risen Christ and the Spirit are identified; but it is true that the appearance of the one is the occasion for the full bestowal of the other (xx, 22). That is not at all inconsistent with the record of *Acts* that there was a signal manifestation of the power of the Spirit at the ensuing feast of Pentecost; indeed the picture of a period of " waiting " after the initial bestowal of the gift, while it worked in the apostolic band like yeast in the dough, till at last it broke forth in a vast release of energy, is psychologically most probable.

Having in mind what happened in that closed room on the evening of the first Easter Day (xx, 22) we need have no difficulty in understanding the close connexion here made between the coming of the Spirit and the coming of Christ. He has spoken of the former, and passes to the latter as something not separable from it. *I will not leave you bereft, I am coming to you.*

The translation " comfortless " with its apparent connexion with " the Comforter " has no warrant in the original. The Lord is going away; but, because He is going to the Father, His going is itself His return. So the moment of separation is the occasion of re-union. In English, the present tense has often a future reference; though this is not impossible in

Greek, it is unusual. The tense here is a genuine present. The going is the coming; consequently as He begins to speak of going, He also says *I am coming to you*. The separation which is imminent will make Him invisible to the world, which will go its way ignoring the manifestations of His presence; but all the while the disciples will be aware of these, and will be taking note of His continued vitality and therein of the promise of their own eternal life. *Yet a little while, and the world taketh note of me no more, but ye take note of me that I live and ye shall live.*

When the disciples come to know their Lord as one " that liveth, and was dead, and is alive for ever-more ", they will also know Him as one that has " the keys of Death and of Hades " (*Revelation* i, 18), so that He can release His own from the grip of death and be to them a source of life. St. John does not encourage either the Greek doctrine of immor-tality nor the Pharisees' hope of a resurrection apart from God's act in and through Christ; eternal life is a gift of God in Christ who is Himself *the Resurrection and the Life* (xi, 25). Our hope of such life is grounded in the knowledge that He lives.

In that day ye will recognise that I am in my Father, and ye in me, and I in you. *In that day* — the day of illumination which the Resurrection would inaugurate. By that illumination we shall recognise the Lord as truly the Mediator. The words used are the fullest expression yet given to that thought. Christ is in the Father; the disciples are in Christ; and Christ is in them. We have already (11) had the declaration that Christ is in the Father and the Father in Him. He is therefore in this double relation of " within-ness " as regards both the Father and His disciples.

This truth is vitally connected with that of the life which He has and which by consequence we hope to have (19); for knowledge of this truth is itself that life (xvii, 3). And it is vitally connected with the love

for Him which issues in observance of His commandments (21); for the "within-ness" asserted is
the perfection of love.

*He that hath my commandments and observeth them,
he it is that loveth me.* Love was spoken of as the
source of obedience (15); now obedience is spoken
of as the test of love. Our love for Christ, won from
us by His love for us, wins love from the Father, and
loving self-manifestation from Christ. *He that loveth
me shall be loved by my Father, and I will love him
and manifest myself to him.* The Father loves all His
children with an infinite love, such love as could be
expressed only by giving His only-begotten Son.
Yet there is a special love also in His heart for those
who love that Son. The universal love of God is not
a featureless uniformity of good-will. Good-will to
all there is; but also for each whatever special quality
of love is appropriate to him; and there must be a
special quality of love for those who love the Son whom
the Father loved *before the foundation of the world*
(xvii, 24). The Son Himself, who is the "express
image" of the Father's universal love, has a special
quality of love (how could it be otherwise?) for those
who love Him in return; and to them He will
manifest Himself.

As we read these words of the Incarnate Word, we
tend to forget that to His disciples He was first and
foremost the Messiah, the inaugurator of the Kingdom
of God. For them this made His words bewildering.
If they had understood the Parable of the Sower it
need not have been so; but though the mystery was
given to them (*St. Mark* iv, 11) they still could not
understand a Kingdom of God which here and there
fails to take root, here and there succeeds for a while,
and only here and there bears fruit. The manifestation of the Son of Man, when it comes, must surely
be to all the world. *There saith to him Judas, not
Iscariot* (we picture the Apostle John dictating to John

the Elder and Evangelist, and when he comes to the word " Judas " the Elder looks up to protest that Judas had gone out; — in answer the words are added *not Iscariot*), "*Lord, what then has happened that thou art about to manifest thyself to us and not to the world?*" *To us:* he claims for the whole band of disciples that they love the Lord, for it is to those who love Him that the promise of the manifestation was given (21). But he is bewildered by the thought of a limited manifestation. How can it be *to us and not to the world?* The Lord gives no direct answer; the question as framed expresses a purely speculative interest, and to such questions the Lord never gives a direct answer, but always points to the moral and spiritual principle involved. Here that principle is the wonder and intimacy of the fellowship with God that results from love of the Lord Jesus. *Jesus answered and said to him, If any man love me, my word he will observe, and my Father will love him, and we shall come to him and make a resting-place with him.* The answer recapitulates the teaching, bringing together the connexion between love and obedience (15, 21), the Father's love for those that love the Son (21), and the fact that the Father and the Son are so united that the action of either is the action also of the other (20), so that the " coming " of Christ (18) is a coming also of the Father: *we shall come.* But to all this an addition is made; as Christ prepares a resting-place for us, that where He is, we also may be (3), so here the love of Him prepares in our hearts a resting-place for Him, and not for Him alone but for the Father also. There is no emphasis here on the resting-place as a temporary abode; but there is clear expression of the thought that the Father and the Son come to the disciple to be his guests. This is a thought even more wonderful than the other. That I should somewhere find a place, a little place, prepared for me in the Father's house is wonderful, but my memory of God's love makes it not incredible. But it would be incredible in any other connexion than that of this divine discourse, that the Father and the Son should come to lodge with me.

> This sanctuary of my soul
>   Unwitting I keep white and whole,
> Unlatched and lit, if Thou should'st care
>   To enter or to tarry there.
>
> With parted lips and outstretched hands
>   And listening ears Thy servant stands,
> Call Thou early, call Thou late,
>   To Thy great service dedicate.[1]

> My spirit longs for Thee
>   Within my troubled breast,
> Though I unworthy be
>   Of so divine a Guest.
>
> Of so divine a Guest
>   Unworthy though I be,
> Yet has my heart no rest
>   Unless it come from Thee.[2]

"Unworthy" indeed; and for that reason the warning must be added. Like all words of divine promise, these are words also of judgement. For we may refuse the promise, and turn away the divine Guests. *He that loveth me not, doth not observe my words; and the word which ye hear is not mine but the Father's who sent me.*

He has led them, and us, to the innermost secret (20) and the ultimate hope (19). That is all that can be done now, apart from some elaboration of the same themes as they make their way to the Garden of Agony ("The Son of Man must suffer") and the exaltation on the Cross. For more than this they must wait for the illumination of the Comforter. *These*

---

[1] Charles Sorley, *Expectans Expectavi.*   [2] Byrom.

things have I spoken to you while abiding with you; but the Comforter — the Spirit, the Holy One — whom the Father will send in my name, he will teach you all things and will bring to your remembrance all things which I said to you.

Here first the Comforter is spoken of as the Holy Spirit, and that solemn title is given in its most formal and emphatic form. It was not an unknown title for the divine Being in His intercourse with man (*Psalm* li, 11; *Isaiah* lxiii, 10). But it was not frequent. Thus it was appropriate as the name for this element within the Godhead which became known through the distinctive Christian experience of relationship to God.

The Holy Spirit is not simply the Creator Spirit as He may be understood apart from Christ, though He is the Creator Spirit. It is only through Christ that we are able to recognise Him (17). The Father sends Him in the Name of the Son; He represents the Son, and His teaching is that of the Son. But it is not limited, as the teaching of the Lord is, by an approaching catastrophe which fixes the end of the period available. He can continue His teaching till all the ground is covered — *He will teach you all things*. Especially will He make those days in Galilee and Jerusalem live again and yield up their secret — *and will bring to your remembrance all things which I said to you*; for He is " the Spirit of Jesus " (*Acts* xvi, 7).

*

The sacred period in the Upper Room has reached its close. The Last Supper has been shared, the Eucharist instituted, the innermost secret declared. It is time for the Lord to start on that last journey of which He has so often spoken. But first He will say farewell.

27-31. " Peace I leave to you, the peace that is mine I give to you. Not as the world gives do I give to you. Let not your hearts be troubled or dismayed. Ye heard that I said to you ' I go away and

I come to you '. If ye loved me ye would have rejoiced that I go to the Father, because the Father is greater than I. And now I have told you before it come to pass, that when it is come to pass ye may believe. No longer shall I speak many things to you, for there cometh the prince of the world, and in me he hath not anything. But that the world may recognise that I love the Father, and that as the Father commanded me thus I do — arise, let us go hence."

Peace. It was the ordinary term of greeting or farewell. But on the lips of Jesus it meant something special. That special gift is His bequest; *peace I leave to you, the peace that is mine I give to you.* He is in the toils of a traitor; His enemies are gathering to destroy Him; and He speaks of *the peace that is mine.* It is an inward peace, independent of circumstance, springing from His union with the Father. This it is which He bequeathes, and which can be ours by His gift if we will receive it.

Not as the world giveth do I give to you. How does the world give? The immediate reference is to the words of salutation, " I give you peace ", which can be no more than a good wish. Christ's bequest of peace is effectual, and actually bestows a permanent possession. Moreover the world gives its best at first and *then that which is worse* (ii, 10), but the " peace of God " is known to those who receive it as deeper and richer and fuller as years pass and the storms of life assail it.

Since our peace is grounded not in circumstance but in the Lord, we should be free from all dismay. So at the close we return to the keynote which had been struck at the outset (1), but here with an added note as well. *Let not your hearts be troubled or dismayed.* The new phrase recalls the charge given to an earlier Jesus, familiar to us as Joshua, on the eve of conquest (*Joshua* i, 9). So, as the later Joshua enters upon the last struggle of His victorious campaign, wherein He will conquer not only a promised land but *the world* itself (xvi, 33, where peace and victory are combined), He bids His followers be free from

perturbation or dismay. The ground of their confidence is to be what He has told them of the goal of
His journey. *Ye heard that I said to you, " I go away
and I come to you ". If ye loved me ye would have
rejoiced that I go to the Father because the Father is
greater than I.* His going and His coming are one
thing, because the goal of His journey is the Father;
to be with the Father is the fulfilment of His being
and that He should go to the Father is the ground of
their hope and strength (12). What matters is that
they, and we, should believe that He is in the Father
and we in Him, and that the mode of this reciprocal
inherence is the sacrifice wherein is manifested the
love which is itself that perfect union. Therefore He
expounds the secret in advance so that the event —
so strange to human thinking (*St. Mark* viii, 33)—may
not destroy their faith but confirm it. *Now I have
told you before it come to pass, that when it is come to pass
ye may believe.*

There is not much opportunity left for teaching.
The world will soon break in upon the companionship
of the little band of friends, and there is nothing in
common between the worldly principle and the Lord.
The force of all that makes *the world* what it is as
a kingdom or system not of God will be put forth
against Him in sheer antagonism; that will be the
opportunity for the supreme proof that He loves the
Father and perfectly obeys Him, a proof that must be
given in action, not in word. *No longer shall I speak
many things to you, for there cometh the prince of the
world, and in me he hath not anything. But that the
world may recognise that I love the Father, and that, as
the Father commanded me, thus I do — arise, let us go
hence.*

So they leave the Upper Room and start to walk
across the Temple Courts towards Kidron and
Gethsemane.

IN THE TEMPLE COURT

Chapters XV, XVI, XVII

In the lighted Upper Room there had been some traces of conversation, and not only continuous discourse. Simon Peter (xiii, 36-38), Thomas (xiv, 5), Philip (xiv, 8), Jude (xiv, 22) are mentioned by name as breaking in with questions or comments. But as the little company moves in the darkness of the night through the city and across the Temple Court no individual disciple intervenes. So far as any speak besides the Lord it is *some of his disciples* (xvi, 17) or *his disciples* (xvi, 29) — a group murmuring their awestruck wonder or assurance.

The first subject of discourse is that union of the disciples with their Lord of which He had spoken earlier (xiv, 20). He now describes it as a living union (xv, 1-10), and goes on to speak of its results, first in the relation of the disciples to their Lord (xv, 11-17), then in the relations of the disciples to the world (xv, 18–xvi, 4). This leads Him to speak more precisely of His departure and the coming of the Comforter (xvi, 5-7), of the Comforter and the world (xvi, 8-11), of the Comforter and the disciples (xvi, 12-15), of sorrow turned to joy (xvi, 16-22), of prayer and its answer (xvi, 23-27), of divine triumph (xvi, 28-33).

We picture the Lord and His disciples leaving the Upper Room with minds full of what had there been done and said. They walk for a time in silence through the dark street, and enter the Temple Court. There in front of them, glinting in the light of the full moon, was the great Golden Vine that trailed over the Temple porch, the type of the life of Israel entwined

about the sanctuary of God. How frequent that
image of the vine or the vineyard had been! It is
enough to recall the " song of my well-beloved touch-
ing his vineyard " (*Isaiah* v, 1-7) or the Psalm about
the vine which the Lord brought out of Egypt
(*Psalm* lxxx, 8-16). Here is that vine in symbol; as
they look at it the Lord begins to speak with a gentle
smile on His lips and hand pointing to the golden
vine — *I am the vine, the true vine.*

E

CHAPTER XV

The Living Union of the Lord and His Disciples

1-10. " I am the vine, the true vine, and my Father is the husbandman. Every branch in me not bearing fruit — he taketh it away; and every branch bearing its fruit — he cleanseth it, that it may bear more fruit. Already ye are clean because of the word which I have spoken to you. Abide in me and I in you. As the branch cannot bear fruit from itself unless it abide in the vine, so neither can ye unless in me ye abide. I am the vine, ye are the branches. He that abideth in me and I in him, he it is that beareth fruit in abundance, because apart from me ye can do nothing. If a man abide not in me, he was cast outside as the branch and was withered; and they gather them and into the fire they cast them and they are burned. If ye abide in me and my sayings abide in you, ask whatsoever ye will and it shall come to pass for you — (In this was glorified my Father — your bearing fruit in abundance) — and ye shall become my disciples. As the Father loved me, I also loved you; abide in the love that is mine. If ye observe my commandments, ye will abide in my love, as I have observed my Father's commandments and abide in his love."

I am the Vine, the true Vine. The vine was a recognised symbol of Israel. But it was employed to represent, as it does in the two passages cited above, Israel's failure. The *true vine* stands for what Israel was called to be. Thus the Lord here proclaims that the purpose of God entrusted to Israel is in fact being fulfilled in Himself. He is the true Israel, the faithful Remnant. He is in His own Person the whole People of God. Though the image was familiar, and its implication is startling, yet it has other special suggestions which are here most appropriate; for the vine lives to give its life-blood. Its flower is small, its fruit abundant; and when that fruit is mature and the vine has for a moment become glorious, the treasure of the grapes is torn down and the vine is cut back to the stem

and next year blooms again,
Not bitter for the torment undergone,
Not barren for the fulness yielded up.

        .   .   .   .   .

The Living Vine, Christ chose it for Himself:—
God gave to man for use and sustenance
Corn, wine, and oil, and each of these is good:
And Christ is Bread of Life and Light of Life.
But yet He did not choose the summer corn,
That shoots up straight and free in one quick growth,
And has its day, and is done, and springs no more:
Nor yet the olive, all whose boughs are spread
In the soft air, and never lose a leaf,
Flowering and fruitful in perpetual peace;
But only this for Him and His in one —
The everlasting, everquickening Vine,
That gives the heat and passion of the world
Through its own life-blood, still renewed and shed.[1]

Those who heard the Lord speak had lately been
in the Upper Room when He handed to them the
Cup of Blessing, saying it was His Blood of the New
Covenant, and that He would not " drink of this fruit
of the Vine ", till the Kingdom of God should be come
(*St. Luke* xxii, 16). Those who transfer this chapter
and the next to the middle of Chapter XIII find in
that Cup the immediate occasion of this saying. We
find its occasion in the Golden Vine on the porch of the
Temple; but the mysterious words so lately spoken
must have been vividly present to the disciples' mind,
and they must recognise that He is here explaining
what so lately He did and said in the Upper Room.

From the dawn of history, even from that twilight
where history, legend and myth are inextricably intermingled, there had been a Community conscious of
divine commission. Its origin is recorded in the Call
of Abraham, in whom all families of the earth should
be blessed (*Genesis* xii, 1-3). If this story represents

[1] Mrs. Hamilton King, *The Disciples*.

rather a tribal migration than an individual adventure, as some scholars think, that sharpens the point of our contention. When history begins, the commissioned community already exists. We trace God's dealings with it as seen and interpreted by Prophets, with their deepening insight into the divine character and purpose. This shews them that the whole People is incapable of making that perfect response which the divine righteousness demands, and that the divine purpose can find fulfilment only in a Remnant. Then even this hope proves too high, and in the culminating intuition of the Old Testament an unknown Prophet perceives that the perfect response will be given and the divine purpose fulfilled by one individual, in whom the whole significance of Israel will be concentrated (*Isaiah* liii). So it came to pass. The Vine that was brought out of Egypt (*Psalm* lxxx, 8; *St. Matthew* ii, 15) is Jesus Himself, *the true vine*. But because He is not merely one of the sons of Abraham, but Himself *before Abraham* (viii, 58) and *one* with *the Father* (x, 30), He is able to incorporate us into Himself so that we become His branches. The Tree that was planted on Calvary has shoots going out into all the world. By perfectly fulfilling the mission of Israel He released it from national limitations, so that from the Cross and Resurrection onwards the Chosen People is the community of those whose hearts have received the divine Word spoken in Him; from that time the Chosen People is the One Man in Christ Jesus (i, 12; *Galatians* iii, 26-28). For His life is offered that it may flow in our veins, that " fruit of the vine " which is the Blood of the New Covenant (*St. Mark* xiv, 24, 25), the love which has conquered death. (Let us here recall vi, 52-58, and the thoughts which it suggested — pp. 94-96.)

My Father is the husbandman. As He was sent by the Father, so the Father has care for Him at all times (xi, 42); but the thought passes at once to the activity in which this care is shewn, and which concerns not the Lord in His own Person but His disciples.

Every branch in me not bearing fruit — *he taketh it away.* The construction requires a pause after the word *fruit.* The possibility of a barren branch is real. The fact that we are " in Christ " does not make us sinless, as St. Paul recognised with vividness and perplexity. We may have been made " members of Christ " in Baptism and yet shew no " fruit of the Spirit ". That is not so terrible a thought where Baptism is administered in infancy; for however difficult that practice is to justify, and we ought to recognise that the justification though abundant is not evident, at least it alleviates the problem of post-baptismal faithlessness. But we are not here concerned with questions of ecclesiastical administration, even the most solemn. There is a profound " mystery of iniquity " here. It is possible to be genuinely drawn to the Lord, to follow His call, to be of His company, and still to bear no fruit. It is possible for a man to betray Him *being one of the Twelve* (vi, 71). When the Lord spoke of Himself as the Bread of Life, Judas was repelled. Before He spoke of Himself as the Vine whose " fruit " is to become our life-blood, Judas had been removed. He was in the Vine, " in Christ ", a branch not bearing fruit; and the Father had taken him away.

Did he not go of his own will, when he went out into the night? Yes, certainly; but that action was no more of his own will than is the action of any who comes to the Lord. Yet this is due to the drawing of the Father (vi, 44). For the action of God is through our wills, and does not override them. He draws us by His love; and men are never so free as when they act from the love in their hearts which love shewn to them has called forth. If, then, I come by my own will yet because the Father draws me, so also it is the Father who is taking me away if I depart by my own will. He offers me the love divine; it draws me or repels me, according to the condition of my will. It had repelled Judas: *after the sop, then entered into him Satan* (xiii, 27). His going was an act of defiance on his part; it was an act of condemnation and execution on the part of God. This is the thought of judgement everywhere presented in this Gospel.

We are in the Vine. Are we bearing fruit? No amount of ascetic discipline or devotional fervour is a substitute for the practical obedience which alone is " fruit ". That obedience however is not a matter of " works ", though these will follow from it, and if they are lacking, there is no " fruit ". Obedience is to God's command; " and this is his commandment, that we should believe the name of his Son Jesus Christ, and love one another even as he gave us commandment " (*I John* iii, 23). If we really " believe the name ", that is accept as true the divine word spoken in Him, and accept as indeed the revelation of God what we see in Him, and if we truly " love one another ", the works will follow without fail. Are we bearing fruit? Or are we ready for nothing but to be taken away by the Husbandman?

Even if we are bearing fruit, there is no ground for contentment; there is still need for the pruning knife of the Husbandman: *every branch bearing its fruit — he cleanseth it, that it may bear more fruit.* That cleansing may be painful. It is almost bound to be. But the pain can be the condition of more abundant fruit.

Pain, considered in isolation, is, no doubt, an evil. But we easily misconceive the problem of pain, as it presents itself to a Christian mind. The world, starting from a crude notion of justice as consisting in a correlation of pain and guilt, as though so much pain could be regarded as wiping out so much guilt, is bewildered by the suffering of the innocent. The Christian has no interest in solving the problem as thus stated ; he must begin by formulating it afresh. For the evil of sin is so great that no amount of pain could ever be regarded as a counter-weight. Of course it is not meant that it is better virtuously to tell the truth and so facilitate a murder than to prevent a murder by telling a lie; but that is because lying with that object is not sin. Sin is the setting by man of his will against God's — consciously (when guilt is also involved) or unconsciously. This is the essential evil; no pain is comparable to it. Consequently, in a world which sin has once entered, no amount of pain can redress the balance and vindicate the justice of the world's order. The problem as stated above arises, not from the facts, but from a bad notion of justice. Pain is in fact evil only in a secondary sense; it is something which, other things being equal, it is right to avoid. But it must always be chosen in preference to moral evil, such as treachery or cruelty; and when it is bravely borne, it has such an effect that we could not wish it away. From a Christian standpoint, the suffering of the innocent is not so great a problem as the suffering of the guilty, or at least very much of it. It is noticeable in war that the suffering of the trenches refines still further the finer natures and brutalises still further the coarser natures. The attachment of mere suffering to crimes may perhaps deter the potential criminal; it seldom reforms the actual criminal. It is harder to see the justification in the eyes of a righteous God of pain which degrades the sufferer, however guilty he may be, than of pain which ennobles the sufferer, however innocent he may be.

It is of ennobling pain that we are thinking here. If we have any ground to hope that we are numbered among the branches which bear fruit, we can welcome every kind of pain that comes to us, knowing that it is capable of rendering us able to *bear more fruit*.

We can make that claim; for the word of Christ

is in our ears; and this is what makes " clean " for the bearing of fruit. *Already ye are clean, because of the word which I have spoken to you.* When He said to Peter *Ye are clean* (xiii, 10), He had not given the ground for that assertion. Now it is plainly stated. The disciples of the Lord are *clean* because they are disciples, hearing His word — the utterance of Him who is the self-utterance of God. But this does not mean either that they are already perfect, or that there is no danger of contamination. The quality of life which springs from discipleship must be maintained and deepened by fellowship with the Lord. So we are led to the words which gather up the whole meaning of what it is to be a Christian.

Abide in me, and I in you. The whole phrase has an imperative tone: let there be mutual indwelling. Of course the command is to the disciple, not to the Lord. *Abide in me,* of which the consequence will be that I shall abide in you; yet the two are not presented as occasion and consequence, but as a twofold condition which we are bidden to bring into existence.

All forms of Christian worship, all forms of Christian discipline, have this as their object. Whatever leads to this is good; whatever hinders this is bad; whatever does not bear on this is futile. This is the life of the Christian: *Abide in me and I in you.* All truth and depth of devotion, all effectiveness in service spring from this. It is not a theme for words but for the deeper apprehensions of silence: *Abide in me and I in you.*

As the branch cannot bear fruit from itself unless it abide in the vine, so neither can ye unless in me ye abide. From itself — as He has used the expression *from myself* (v, 30; vii. 17) in order to repudiate the thought that He is Himself the origin of His words and actions, so here He says of the disciple, who is a branch in the vine, that the source of his fruitfulness is not in himself the branch, but in the vine of which he is one part. The disciple makes no claim to originality; his one aim is to let the life of the Lord, in whom he abides, and who abides in him, find expression through him. The subtle alteration in the order of words in the two parallel phrases emphasises the utter completeness of our dependence, which will be still more starkly expressed in the next verse.

I am the Vine. Here is the last of the sevenfold declarations of His Person, beginning with the words of the Divine Name, I AM; and it sums up all the rest. He is Himself the fellowship in which eternal life is found, and that life is His life.

I am the Vine, ye the branches. He does not say that He is the stem and we the branches, though He, and none other, is the stem. So when St. Paul uses the parable of the body, sometimes Christ is the whole Body (*I Corinthians* xii, 12, 27) and sometimes the Head (*Ephesians* iv, 15). No other is the stem of the Vine; no other is the Head of the Body. Yet it does not express the whole relation of the Lord to His disciples to say that He is the stem and they the branches, or that He is the Head and they the limbs. He is the whole Vine, the whole Body, and we, as branches or limbs, are " very members incorporate " in Him.

This language cannot be used concerning the relation of any human leader to his followers without such exaggeration as to be ludicrous. It can only be appropriate if He of whom it is used is that infinite Spirit " in whom we live and move and have our being ". The tone of the discourse is here tender and intimate, not (as in Chapter VIII) severe and judicial; but the claim made by Christ concerning His own status is as great. We find the same transition from the claim " All things have been delivered unto me of my Father " to the invitation " Come unto me . . . and I will give you rest ", where the invitation is justified only if the claim is true (*St. Matthew* xi, 27 and 28).

He that abideth in me and I in him — he it is that beareth fruit in abundance. Here is the answer to our question " How? " when we hear the precept " make the tree good " (*St. Matthew* xii, 33). Our discipline is not a bracing of our wills to conformity with a law; it is the maintenance of communion with the Lord to the point of mutual indwelling. This so purifies the heart that at last there is no need for any deliberate control of desire, because desire itself is sanctified. But though our discipline is not conformity with a code, it is obedience to a commandment; for " this is his commandment, that we should believe the name of his Son Jesus Christ and love one another, even as he gave us commandment " (*I John* iii, 23). The commandment is not primarily to " do " this or that, but to trust and to love, as appears very plainly in verses 8 to 12, to which we are coming.

Apart from me ye can do nothing. " Works done before the grace of Christ and the Inspiration of His Spirit are not pleasant to God, forasmuch as they spring not of faith in Jesus Christ, neither do they make men meet to receive grace or (as the School authors say) deserve grace of congruity: yea rather, for that they are not done as God hath willed and commanded them to be done, we doubt not but they have the nature of sin." Article XIII states the matter in the unsympathetic tone born of theological controversy; but what it says is true. " The nature of sin " is self-centredness — the putting of self in the centre where God alone should be. We are all born doing this; that is Original Sin. From this condition there may be partial deliverance through devotion to scientific truth or artistic beauty or patriotic loyalty. But such deliverance is only partial. In all my strivings to attain some ideal or perform some service, unless my heart and will are wholly captivated, there will be some self-assertion, and probably a great deal. That is why the consciously virtuous person is disagreeable. It is not virtue that can save the world or any one in it, but love. And love is not at our command. We cannot generate it from within ourselves. We can win it only by surrender to it. The " strong man armed " of our self-complacency is secure until the " stronger than he " cometh (*St. Luke* xi, 21 and 22). There will be no full surrender except to the perfect manifestation of perfect love, that is to say to Jesus Christ come in the flesh. But He makes Himself known in fact in other ways besides His incarnate life; so far as it is to the Divine Self-Utterance or Word in truth or beauty or goodness that men open their hearts, their works are done through " the grace of Jesus Christ and the Inspiration of His Spirit ". That may be a real surrender, but not complete; therefore those works, while not mere sins, yet have some of " the nature of sin " about them.

We cannot too strongly or harshly drive this truth into our souls, however eager we may be to trace " the grace of Jesus Christ " in others, even in atheists. Apart from Him, I can do nothing. All fruit that I ever bear or can bear comes wholly from His life within me. No particle of it is mine as distinct from His. There is, no doubt, some part of His whole purpose that He would accomplish through me; that is my work, my fruit, in the sense that I, and not another, am the channel of His life for this end; but in no other sense. Whatever has its ultimate origin in myself is sin: " O God, forasmuch as without thee we are not able to please thee, mercifully grant that thy Holy Spirit may in all things direct and rule our hearts, through Jesus Christ our Lord ".

If a man abide not in me, he was cast outside as the branch, and was withered; and they gather them and into the fire they cast them and they are burned. The violent change of tense — an idiom that cannot be reproduced in good English but which is repeated in this translation for the challenge which it offers — indicates the fact that the penalty and the severance from Christ are simultaneous, for indeed they are identical. It is not said that if we do not abide in Christ we shall subsequently or ultimately be cast out of the vineyard on to the fire; what is said is that our failure to abide in Him is, there and then, that rejection and destruction. As the labourers gather the branches that are broken off and dried up, and toss them out to be burnt, so is already the lot of any disciple who fails to abide in his Lord. The devout Jews who heard the words were familiar with the passage which suggested them. Ezekiel had pointed out that the wood of the vine is useless, and is " given to the fire for fuel ". As a channel for the life of the vine, the branch has use and bears fruit; separated from the vine it is worthless: " shall wood be taken thereof to make any work? or will men take a pin of it to hang any vessel thereon? " (*Ezekiel* xv, 2-4). So useless is the disciple who has become severed from his Lord.

It need not be so. *If ye abide in me and my sayings abide in you, ask whatsoever ye will and it shall come to pass for you — and ye shall become my disciples.* He had already said *If ye ask anything in my name, I will do it* (xiv, 13 and 14). To ask in His name is to ask as His representative, or in other words, according to His will. We acknowledge Him as the source of the blessing, so that its bestowal will bind us more closely to Him, not make us forgetful of Him; and as what is asked is what He already desires to give, the gift follows upon the fulfilment of this condition. Here we are taught how the condition may be fulfilled. How can I, in practice, ask in Christ's name or as His representative? Only if I am abiding in Him

and His *sayings* abide in me. It is through His sayings
that this mutual indwelling is effected. We do well
to remember that our Lord is much more than a
teacher. But a teacher He is; and it is through
His teaching that our minds receive His mind so that
we may become one with Him and He with us. In one
sense this is itself the culmination and fruit of discipleship; it is so, if the mutual indwelling is complete.
That perfection is not reached on earth, and the reward
of discipleship is to become more fully disciples, as
we receive *of His fulness* and *grace for grace* (i, 16).

Inserted into this sequence of thought is a paren-
thesis, lest we should for a moment suppose that it
is possible to ask in Christ's name for the satisfaction
of our own desires; all that we can ask in His name
is that we may really do His will and bear fruit for
the Lord of the vineyard. We ask whatsoever we will;
but being in Christ our will must be for the glory of
God and the accomplishment of His purpose. Therefore the coming to pass of what we ask is the glorification of God and the bearing of abundant fruit; *It shall
come to pass for you: in this was glorified my Father,
your bearing fruit in abundance.* Our fruitfulness is
due to God's activity released or called forth by our
prayer.

Here we have a searching test of our prayer-life.
Is it fruitful — in the effectiveness of our intercessions
or our own growth in grace? If not, it is because
we are not praying in His name; and that, again, is
because we are not abiding in Him nor His sayings
in us. If we really so abide, we shall not only desire
His will to be done rather than what would have been
our own, but we shall know what it is. So often we
get far enough to prefer His will to ours in principle;
but we are not in communion with Him close enough
to avoid insisting upon our judgement of what His will
must be — like Peter at Caesarea Philippi or at the
feet-washing. We will follow Him. . . . But surely

He does not mean to go that way. . . . It leads to certain failure. It leads to a Cross.

There is a most subtle danger of a revival of self-will in the very act of surrendering it. The only safeguard is to abide in Him in still closer communion, still deeper love — love like His.

As the Father loved me I also loved you. Again we find the doctrine of mediation, but for the first time in terms of love. It is a perfect love that has been given to us; it is nothing less than the love which unites the Father and the Son in the very Godhead itself, and which is the Holy Spirit. This perfect love is " bestowed upon us " through Christ. *Abide in the love that is mine.* The words mean much more than " continue in the shelter of my love for you " (Bernard). The divine love, which is the Holy Ghost, is much more than a sheltering protection; rather it is a pervasive atmosphere in which we may dwell, and which we may breathe, so that it becomes the breath of our lives (cf. xx, 22). We are to let that love wrap us about, enfolding us in its embrace. How do we do this? *If ye observe my commandments, ye will abide in my love, as I have observed my Father's commandments and abide in His love.* We hold ourselves in that love by obedience; and the love is the power in which we obey. He had said *If ye love me, ye will observe my commandments* (xiv, 15); now He says *If ye observe my commandments, ye will abide in my love.* Love and obedience are two parts of one relationship — the relationship of creature to Creator, of child to Father, of sinner to Redeemer. Is my obedience defective? — let me kindle my love by communion with the Lord. Is my love feeble? Let me deepen communion by deliberate obedience. But what kind of obedience is it? Are we to " do " this, and avoid " doing " that? No; that is the way of the law and its works. Our obedience is to the commandments of the Lord, which are — to trust God and to love

Him (12; cf. vi, 29; xiii, 34; *I John* iii, 23).

The pattern once again is the perfect love within the Being of God, not this time the love of the Father for the Son, but the perfect obedience of the Son to the Father and the love which is in that obedience expressed and actualised. The divine perfection is our model and standard; and all that falls short of it is sin (*St. Matthew* v, 45 and 48; *Romans* iii, 23).

*

THE RELATION OF THE DISCIPLES TO THE LORD

11-17. " These things have I spoken unto you that the joy which is mine may be in you and that your joy may be fulfilled. This is the commandment which is mine, that ye love one another as I loved you. Greater love than this hath no man, that a man lay down his life on behalf of his friends. Ye are my friends, if ye do what I command you. No longer do I call you slaves; for the slave knoweth not what his lord doeth; but you I have called friends, because all things which I heard from my Father, I made known to you. Not you chose me, but I chose you, and appointed you that ye may go your ways and bear fruit, and that your fruit may abide, that what- soever ye ask the Father in my name, he may give it you. These things I command you, that ye love one another."

The joy that is mine: the joy of unbroken communion with the Father; the joy of a world by Him redeemed from selfishness and mutual destruction to love and abundant life; the " joy that was set before Him " (*Hebrews* xii, 2). The promise and hope is not only that we may be joyful as our Master is joyful — (my joy) — but that joy of the same substance and quality as His — *the joy which is mine* — may be in us.

Evidently that joy is no external happiness, nor can it be produced by any circumstances. It is a state of the soul. It is the condition of the soul that is filled with love, as joy comes next to love in the fruitage of the Spirit (*Galatians* v, 22. N.B.: that catalogue of graces is not a list of " fruits of the Spirit " but an articulation of the one and indivisible " fruit of the Spirit" which is the surrender of the soul to God under the impulse of His revealed love). The joy which is Christ's can only be known by those who, with Him, are obedient to the divine command and responsive to the divine teaching. So He gives His command and His teaching in order that the joy which is His may be in us.

It is no alien gift; it is the completion of our own and our only true joy — *and that your joy may be fulfilled*. For we too were made in the image of God, who is Love. That image in us is distorted and defaced; for we are self-centred and not perfect in love. Yet we can " reflect as a mirror the glory of the Lord " (*II Corinthians* ii, 18); and He who is the " express image " of God's substance (*Hebrews* i, 3) is that image which we were created to bear. This call, against which our self-centredness rebels, is the call to be our real selves. The call to the pain of self-sacrifice is also, and more deeply, the call to the fulfilment of our joy.

Corresponding to *the joy which is mine* is *the commandment which is mine*. All His commands are gathered up in this. It had been given before (xiii, 34) in close association with His self-offering to death, when He let the traitor go and thereafter in symbol broke His Body and gave to the disciples His Blood, that is to say His life offered in sacrifice. Now He repeats it with the same reference — *that ye love one another as I loved you*. The words which follow shew that His love is to be measured by His death. Love such as that, love to the point of sacrifice even of life, is to be the bond between His disciples. This is not a command to all the world, as will appear very soon (18); nor is it a command concerning the relation of Christians to non-Christians. It is the command to the Christian fellowship. That fellowship owes its existence and quality to the love of Christ. He has drawn us, each one, to Himself; our discipleship is

His doing, not ours (16); in the fellowship which we have, each one, with Him we are in fellowship with one another; and this latter fellowship must be the sphere or arena of a love such as created it. The life of the Vine must be in the branches, making of them all a single organism; the Spirit of Christ must be in the members, making them all one body, and that body His.

Do we feel such a bond with our fellow-Christians? Is our fellowship in Christ a reality more profound and effective than our membership of our earthly fellowships — family, school, party, class, nation, race — and able in consequence to unite us in love across all natural divisions and hostilities? Of course not. And the reason is that we do not truly abide in Him. If we did, His life of sacrificial love would flow through us all and unite us in the most intimate bonds. What is called the Oecumenical Movement[1] represents a dawning consciousness of this truth.

That this mutual love of Christians, reproducing their Lord's love for them, is to be measured by His death is now made perfectly clear. *Greater love than this hath no man, that a man lay down his life on behalf of his friends.* Some have said, is it not greater love to die for enemies than for friends? But this over-stresses the word *friends*. It does not here represent those who love Him but those whom He loves; the saying declares that love has no more complete expression than death on behalf of those to whom it is directed; the distinction between those who return that love and those who do not, does not arise. Love unto death is a complete self-giving; that is what Christ

[1] This is the name given to the various enterprises in which the several Churches are invited to co-operate, and for the most part do co-operate, with the one great exception of the Church of Rome. The two chief enterprises of this sort are the Faith and Order Movement and the Life and Work Movement. Both of these held Conferences — at Edinburgh and Oxford respectively — in Great Britain in 1937. One result of these is an attempt to establish a " World Council of Churches ".

F

endured for His disciples; that is what Christians must be ready to endure for their fellow-Christians.

Yet that love demands and deserves response. When Christ died, it was for those whom He loved; the supreme wonder is that it was for those who did not (as yet) love Him. " God commendeth his own love toward us, in that, while we were yet sinners, Christ died for us " (*Romans* v, 8). But though as objects of His love sinners are truly called His friends, yet they are not all that this name should mean while they are content to remain sinners; if they are to be real friends they must obey the commands: *Ye are my friends if ye do what I command you.* So once more love and obedience are brought together as in xiv, 15 and 21 and xv, 10. But now we learn something more about the quality of our obedience.

The use of the word *friends* has carried the thought on from the relation of the disciples to one another to their relation with their Lord, in which their relation to one another is grounded. *No longer do I call you slaves, for the slave knoweth not what his lord doeth; but you I have called friends, because all things which I heard from my Father, I made known to you.* To St. Paul this seemed to be the very essence of the transition from the Pharisaic Judaism in which he was brought up to faith in God through Jesus Christ: " Ye received not the spirit of slavery again unto fear; but ye received the spirit of adoption whereby we cry Abba, Father " (*Romans* viii, 15). What is the spirit of slavery? The slave, who is only a slave, and not also a friend as some slaves were, has his orders and obeys them, perhaps hoping for reward if he does this well, certainly fearing punishment if he does it ill or not at all. He does not care for the feelings of his master. His only concern is what his master may do to him. Such seems to St. Paul, looking back, to have been his state as a Pharisee. (No doubt like all persons who have suffered sudden conversion he exaggerates the remoteness of his former from his latter state; we may be quite sure that Saul of Tarsus had some quite real love of God in his heart.) But the disclosure, in the life and death of Jesus, of what God's love for us really is had won from him a response which makes him feel no longer like a slave before his master but like a child before his father. He no longer thinks — " this is the command of God which I must obey ", but — " this is God my Father whom I wish to please ". The difference is made by the completeness with which the mind and heart of the Father are disclosed to us in Christ — *all things which I heard from my Father I made known to you.* We are taken into confidence; we are enabled to understand; and what we understand is a wisdom and a love to which we long to trust ourselves in overflowing gratitude and whole-hearted surrender.

Our action is all response; all initiative is with the Lord: *Not ye chose me, but I chose you.* That is fundamental. " Herein is love, not that we loved God, but that he loved us " (*I John* iv, 10). Those of us who were baptised as infants are without excuse if we forget this. Our being Christians is no doing of ours, any more than our being civilised; it is something done to us and for us, not by us, though we have to make appropriate response in the form of obedience prompted by love.

I chose you and appointed you that ye may go your ways and bear fruit and that your fruit may abide. We were chosen first and foremost for fellowship with Christ — " that they might be with him " (*St. Mark* iii, 14); that is our first duty, to abide in Him. But He chose us also to send us forth as His witnesses — " and that he might send them forth to make the proclamation " (*St. Mark, ibid.*). The word which I have translated *go your ways* is that which at the end of the story of the raising of Lazarus I translated (with Bernard) *go home* (xi, 44). It suggests going about one's business, whatever that may be. It is in doing that that we are to *bear fruit*, fruit that will abide. A real Christian, who abides in Christ and Christ in him, exerts an influence among his companions at work or play, in mine or shop or factory or directors' meeting or Parliament, that nothing effaces. But there is more still than this. Such a man becomes a channel through whom the love of God may flow in blessing wheresoever he directs his attention — *and that whatsoever ye ask the Father in my name, he may give it you.* The range of a Christian's fruitful activity is far greater through his prayer, that is the direction of his will, surrendered as it is to God, than through his conduct or direct influence. This is true so far, and only so far, as he prays *in the name* of Christ — that is (as we saw) as His representative; and this we can do only if we abide in Him and His sayings abide in us (7).

Those who do this are a family united in a love which flows through them all, a community of love. So once more the summary is given: *These things I command you, that ye (may) love one another.* To insert that word *may* is to exaggerate the suggestion of purpose and consequence; yet that suggestion is there. Mutual love is the content of the command; it is also the result of obeying it. For the command is also *Abide in me.*

Abide in me; Love one another: these are not two things, but one thing with two aspects, whereof the former is the occasion of the latter. To do this is veritably to participate in the Holy Communion.

*

THE RELATION OF THE DISCIPLES TO THE WORLD

xv, 18–xvi, 4. " If the world hate you, recognise that it hath hated me before you. If ye were from the world, the world would love its own. But because ye are not from the world, but I chose you

out from the world, therefore the world hateth you. Be mindful of
the word which I said to you ' The slave is not greater than his lord '.
If they persecuted me, you also will they persecute; if they observed
my word, yours also will they observe.   But all these things they
will do to you for my Name's sake, because they know not him that
sent me.   If I had not come and spoken to them, they would not
have had sin; but as it is they have no excuse for their sin. He that
hateth me hateth my Father also.   If I had not done among them
works which no one else did, they would not have had sin; but
as it is they have both seen and hated both me and my Father.
But that the word written in their law may be fulfilled — They
hated me without cause.   When the Comforter cometh, whom I
will send to you from the Father, the Spirit of Truth who proceedeth from the Father, he shall bear witness concerning me; and
ye also bear witness because from the beginning ye are with me.
These things have I spoken to you that ye be not overthrown. They
will excommunicate you; indeed there cometh an hour when whosoever killeth you will think he offers worship to God. And these
things will they do because they did not recognise the Father nor
me.   But these things have I spoken to you that, when their hour
cometh, ye may be mindful of them, that I myself told you."

If the world hate you. They would soon know
whether it did or not. That heathen world was bound
to hate the infant Church which stood for principles
so radically opposed to its own. We live in a country
where for many generations the Gospel and the faith
which it calls forth have influenced the lives and
thoughts of men. It is possible that even complete
loyalty to Christ would not win its hatred; and
certainly we must not suppose that in such a country
ecclesiastical persons or assemblies are more sure to
be true to the principles of Christ than are secular
persons and assemblies discharging their proper
responsibilities. Yet that disciple or that Church,
which finds that all men speak well of him or of it, has
cause for anxiety. " The kingdom of this world " is
not yet become " the kingdom of our Lord and of
His Christ " (*Revelation* xi, 15) even in lands called
Christian. The true disciple still offers to the world
a challenge, which it will take up if his faithfulness
is active. Not all that the world hates is good

Christianity; but it does hate good Christianity and always will.

That hatred of the world is hard to face. The world is the most dangerous of the three great enemies. In our conflict with the flesh and the devil the world itself in a civilised country gives us some support. But against the world we must stand alone with our fellow-Christians. If we waver, it must steady us to *recognise* that the world hated our Master before us. It is natural rather than strange that we should stand where He stood, if we *abide in* Him; and that sets us on the other side of a strongly marked dividing line running between us and the world.

If ye were from the world, the world would love its own. It is a question of affinity or the lack of it — not of reasoned attachment or alienation. *From the world*; the phrase suggests a character due to origin (cf. viii, 23). Are we not from the world? Is not that our origin, and do not our characters correspond? Yes — far too largely. But that is not the distinctive and most fundamental fact about us if we are disciples at all. *Because ye are not from the world, but I chose you out from the world:* the phrase *from the world* is repeated, but with a difference. Coupled with the verb *chose out* it no longer represents origin and growth in congruity with that origin, but a place of departure and consequent separation. This is, in part, the occasion of the hate which the world feels. It would not hate angels for being angelic; but it does hate men for being Christians. It grudges them their new character; it is tormented by their peace; it is infuriated by their joy. They belong to it by nature; and they have found in a place where " no sane man " [1] would look for it exactly what the world vainly desires; they must be impostors and deceivers (vii, 12; cf. *II Corinthians* vi, 8). The world, with its serious work to do, has no patience with such char-

[1] See Robert Browning's *Cleon*, the last line.

latans. So we must *be mindful* of His saying (xiii, 16) " *The slave is not greater than his lord* ". When spoken earlier it had conveyed an exhortation to aim at a humility corresponding to that of the Lord who washed His disciples' feet; here it conveys a warning to expect and accept from the world no better treatment than it gave to their Lord — *If they persecuted me, you also will they persecute.* But there is comfort too in the obverse of this — *If they observed my word, yours also will they observe.* In any case, whatever befalls the disciple comes upon him because, and in so far as, he is the representative of his Master: *all these things they will do to you for my Name's sake, because they know not him that sent me.* The disciple represents Christ: Christ represents the Father. If the world could understand that the mission of Christ is divine, it would not persecute His representatives. The word *know* is that which stands for scientific knowledge or accurate information, not that which stands for personal acquaintance; *they know not him that sent me* therefore means " they know not that I came forth from the Father " (see xvi, 28). To recognise this, for almost any reason, is the first stage of Christian faith; for it leads to reverent attention to the Lord and thus at length to that recognition of Him (xiv, 9) which culminates in the vision of the Father in and through Him, and thus again to true knowledge of the Father Himself which is eternal life (xvii, 3 — where the word for *know* is that signifying personal acquaintance).

The coming of the Lord, of which the purpose is always and only to save men from sin, has the inevitable result of revealing their sin, and even intensifying it if they refuse to be won from it. *If I had not come and spoken to them, they would not have had sin, but as it is they have no excuse for their sin.* The teaching of the Lord has the same effect as the Law, which also was from God; it revealed to the dormant conscience the

sin that was already there, and it provoked the uncon-
verted will to vigorous obstinacy in its sin (*Romans*
vii, 7-12). Jews who were loyal to their tradition, the
noblest religious tradition in the world, might still be
involved in what theologians call " material sin " so
far as that tradition was less than the perfect will of
God; but they were not involved in " formal sin ",
which is deliberate action in opposition to that will
made known. Now that it is made known and they
refuse it, the sin becomes inexcusable. For antagonism
to Christ is antagonism to God: *he that hateth me
hateth my Father also.*

Perhaps it may be said that they were still not
guilty of " formal sin ", for that is defiance of conscience. But there is a sin which may not be in that
sense " formal sin " and yet involves guilt as only
" formal sin " is generally supposed to do. This
deeper sin is the sin of the darkened conscience (*St.
Matthew* vi, 23), which prevents men from seeing
goodness when it is before their eyes. *If I had not done
among them the works which no one else did, they would
not have had sin; but as it is they have both seen and
hated both me and my Father.* These works, wherein
power is active in manifest subjection to love, are
" signs " of the divine presence and activity in Him.
Failure to read those signs argues a profound darken-
ing of the conscience. At one time His enemies had
said of such a work — a plainly good work — that it
was done by diabolic power; and He had answered
that this argued such insensitiveness to the very Spirit
of Holiness as to put him who had sunk to it outside
the reach of the divine forgiveness (*St. Matthew* xii,
22-32). Pure goodness has been in action before
their eyes, and they have repudiated it. There was
never a more utterly gross delusion than that " We
needs must love the highest when we see it ", unless
by " see it " we understand " see it for what it is ".
They have both seen and hated both me and my Father.

What more or worse can be said? Yet it is only the
extreme form of a spiritual reality common enough
and recognised by the Psalmists (*Psalms* xxxv, 19 and
lxix, 4).[1] We shall not, perhaps, ever allow ourselves
to hate Christ and His Cross as historically presented;
we very easily hate His call to the Cross when it comes
to ourselves to-day.

Suddenly, as though this terrible thought of hating
the Lord and His Father had recalled the Holy Spirit
against whom that hatred is blasphemy, the Person of
the Comforter is introduced. The world in its blind
sin may persecute and hate; but the Spirit will bear
His own witness. *When the Comforter cometh, the
Spirit of Truth who proceedeth from the Father, whom I
will send to you from the Father, he shall bear witness
concerning me.*

The Son sends the Comforter. The coming of the
Holy Spirit in power is due to the action of the Son
in revealing the love of the Father, and (as we shall
see more clearly) one way of summarising the purpose
of Christ's coming is to say that He came in order
that the Spirit might come. That inward power of
God converting desire itself is a result of the disclosure of the love of God and the response which it
wins. So the Son is the cause of the Spirit's coming;
He sends Him. Yet it is no less true that the Spirit
proceedeth from the Father; because the Father is infinite
love the personal activity of that love ever goes forth.
Not only in Jesus Christ does *the Spirit of Truth* touch
the hearts of men. He spoke to and through Plato,
as the early Christian Fathers fully recognised; and
has spoken through many a seer, poet and prophet
both within and outside the Canon of Holy Scripture.
Wherever there is response in the hearts of men to the
manifested glory of God, whether that manifestation
be in nature or in history, there the Spirit of Truth is

[1] " They that hate me without a cause " (cf. cix, 3, " For the love
that I had unto them, lo, they take now my contrary part ").

at work. He inspires all Science and all Art, and speaks in the conscience of the heathen child. Yet it is also true that the Son sends Him. For only in the Word made flesh is the glory of God truly displayed. *We beheld his glory* (i, 14); that is the condition of receiving the Holy Spirit in His power. He " proceedeth from the Father and (or through) the Son ".

The Spirit of Truth — as contrasted with the false prejudice which led the Jews to hate the highest when they saw it. The Gospel is not a call to feed the soul on lofty ideals which may have no counterpart in reality. It is the proclamation of the truth about God and the world. Every sincere seeker after truth is entitled to claim Christ's authority for saying that he is upheld by the Holy Spirit; for that is implied in this title *the Spirit of truth*. But if he is sincere he will also recognise that he cannot claim that authority unless he also acknowledges that the primary concern of *the Spirit of truth* is to *bear witness concerning* Jesus Christ. For He is the very truth of God, the Eternal Word or self-utterance of the Father.

He shall bear witness concerning me; and ye also bear witness. Co-witnesses with the Holy Ghost: that is the calling of Christian disciples; that is our calling. St. Peter would accept that august position: " We are witnesses of these things; and so is the Holy Ghost whom God hath given to them that obey him " (*Acts* v, 32). The first disciples were qualified for this by their companionship with the Lord from the first days of the ministry: *ye also bear witness, because from the beginning ye are with me.*

We were baptised in infancy; we were (by God's great mercy and election) brought up in Christian homes. Not from the beginning of His ministry, but from the beginning of our lives, we are with Him. What is our witness worth? Does it qualify us to be co-witnesses with the Holy Ghost?

These things have I spoken unto you that ye be not

overthrown. The coming persecution would be a very severe trial to faith, not only because it would test courage and men might deny their allegiance to the Lord from weakness and cowardice, but also because it is hard to believe that a cause is truly God's when it seems to meet with no success, and all power is on the other side. *Overthrown*: it is notoriously hard to represent in English the Greek word translated in the Authorised Version " offended " and in the Revised " made to stumble "; it stands for a failure due to obstacles put in the way, as contrasted with failure due to disloyalty. If the disciples can remember *these things*—the Lord's prediction of the persecution and, no less, His promise of the Comforter, they will find in them the needed safeguard.

They will excommunicate you: the loyal disciple will be attacked through his religious tradition and association. He will have to maintain his constancy in face of the assurance of his fellows that he is pursuing a course hateful to God. So sure of this will they be that *whosoever killeth you will think he offers worship to God.* They will not only think that in persecuting the disciples they are serving God's purpose in the world, but even that they are therein offering worship; the execution will be carried out in the spirit of a ritual sacrifice. It is this religious conscientiousness of the persecutor which makes him so relentless, and also tests so searchingly the faith of his victim. *And these things will they do because they did not recognise the Father nor me.* The revelation was offered, but they were blind to it. They did not " behold His glory ". In Christ the Father was manifested, but they could not recognise either the Father so manifested or the Son as manifesting Him.

But these things have I spoken to you that, when their hour cometh, ye may be mindful of them, that I myself told you. Their hour: the hour of their fulfilment. Then the disciples would look back and say, " This is

what He told us to expect; His word is fulfilled ".
Thus an experience otherwise calculated to assault
faith from without and to undermine it from beneath,
will be converted into an evidence and support of
faith by the realisation that it is a fulfilment of the
Lord's own word.

CHAPTER XVI

(1) THE DEPARTURE OF THE LORD AND THE COMING OF THE COMFORTER

5-7. "These things I did not tell you from the beginning because I was with you. But now I go my way to him that sent me, and none of you asketh me, Whither goest thou? But because I have said these things to you, sorrow hath filled your heart. But I tell you the truth; it is expedient for you that I go away. For if I go not away, the Comforter will not come to you, but if I depart I will send him to you."

WHILE the Lord was with them there was no need to speak of *these things* — persecution for His Name's sake, and the coming of the Comforter. For in those days any persecution that arose was directed against Himself, not against them; and while He was with them, the Comforter would not come (7). But now He is leaving them so far as concerns visible presence, and both warning and promise are in place.

I go my way to him that sent me. The words are repeated from vii, 33, but there they follow the saying *Yet a little while I am with you.* Here, for that phrase the word *Now* is substituted. The sacrifice which is at once the separation of death and the perfecting of union with the Father is at hand. It is the supreme moment of His life and ministry; yet the disciples are not thinking of what it means for Him; their thoughts are all of what it means for themselves. *None of you asketh me, " Whither goest thou? "* St. Peter had asked precisely that, when the Lord had said He was going to a place where they could not follow (xiii, 36); there self-concern prompted the question; here it stifles it. The Lord has now told them the goal of His journey — the Father; but instead of wondering what the joy of that attainment must be, they are brooding over their own imminent loss and the persecutions which they have been warned to expect: *Because I have said these things to you, sorrow hath filled your heart.*

But I tell you the truth; it is expedient for you that I go away. Even from the standpoint of their own interest they should rejoice rather than feel sorrow: *it is expedient for you that I go away.* How could that possibly be true? We look back and think that there was never any privilege like theirs. They had walked with Him in the corn-fields, and sat with Him in the boat upon the lake; they had supped with Him among His friends. What greater privilege could there ever be? Yes — it was a supreme privilege. But what became of that faith which relied upon the Lord as an external Presence to whom they could turn at every moment of doubt or need? When the crisis came it all went to pieces. "They all left him and fled" (*St. Mark* xiv, 50). Simon Peter did indeed follow — " afar off " (*St. Mark* xiv, 54) — to the place where he would stand and warm himself, and say " I know not this man " (*St. Mark* xiv, 71). Yet a few weeks later these same men are found confronting the rulers of their nation with a calm and unruffled courage, and " rejoicing that they were counted worthy to suffer dishonour for the Name " (*Acts* v, 41; cf. also (e.g.) v, 27-32). What explains the transformation? Of course it is that of which the Lord here speaks; He has withdrawn from them as a visible, external Presence, to return in the Person of the Spirit as the very breath of their lives (see xx, 22).

This hard saying states in its most signal instance the fundamental principle of true education. The task of the teacher is to prepare the pupil for the time of separation, which must come, so that the pupil may find within himself such resources as enable him to follow the direction in which the teacher has started him without any further aid. It is not only that the time of separation must come; it is a good thing that it should come, for otherwise that inward strength, which it is the purpose of education to develop, will never be exercised.

We tend to think of that inward strength as our own, and of our trust in it as self-reliance. But it is not our own. Even apart from religion, the inner quality in which we place our trust is the deposit of the tradition in which we were brought up, of the influence of parents and teachers. We could not civilise ourselves. If we had been carried off in infancy to live among savages, we should be savages now. " What hast thou that thou didst not receive? " (*I Corinthians* iv, 7). Of all the boons of civilisation the giver is God; and we lose both some of their value, and an added ground for faith, if we forget this.

In the spiritual life it is of urgent importance that we remember from whom our strength comes — the Holy Spirit, the " Giver of Life ". He is the Spirit of Christ, whom disciples receive through their companionship with Christ. Christ is therefore in that sense the source or sender of the Spirit. He withdraws His visible presence; but He does not *leave us desolate* (xiv, 18); on the contrary, He makes our loss into a blessing. *If I go not away, the Comforter will not come to you, but if I depart I will send him to you.*

*

(2) THE COMFORTER AND THE WORLD

8-11. " And when he is come he will convict the world in respect of sin and of righteousness and of judgment: of sin, in that they believe not on me; and of righteousness in that to the Father I go my way and no longer do ye take note of me; and of judgment in that the prince of this world hath been judged."

The Comforter has a relationship to the world as well as to the disciples, and this is mentioned briefly so that the way may be clear for the description of His work among the disciples, upon which most emphasis is to be laid. But though the reference to His task for the world is brief it is almost infinitely pregnant. As we are still in large measure " of the world " and not yet wholly disciples, it is well for us to draw out the meaning of these close-packed phrases.

He will convict the world. The word translated *convict* means primarily to cross-examine with a view to refutation or conviction, or to bring forward evidence that proves guilt. (The corresponding noun is used in *Hebrews* xi, 1, where it is said that " faith is the *testing* of things not seen ", though there the suggestion is that the unseen forces will meet the test.) The Comforter will bring evidence to prove the world wrong in certain respects. What respects are these? — the three matters most important to man's life, sin, righteousness and judgement. What then is the evidence that He will bring? In respect of sin, it is that men do not believe on Christ; in respect of righteousness, it is that Christ goes to the Father; in respect of judgement, it is that in the Life and Death of Christ the Prince of this world is under judgement.

We may interpret this at two levels — the more obvious and the more profound. Men's failure to believe on Christ is proof of the world's sin; Christ's going to the Father is proof of His righteousness; and the judgement upon the Prince of this world is proof that judgement is operative. All this is true and important; but it does not begin to satisfy the meaning of the words used; and after all it was not by any means evident that the Prince of this world was under judgement in the Passion of Christ.

Let us by all means take to ourselves the lessons of this more obvious interpretation. Our failure to believe — whether absolute or partial — is indeed proof of sin in us, and should stir us to a penitent longing for fuller faith. The Ascension of Christ is

indeed a seal set on His life as a manifestation of
righteousness, and we may learn from Him what
righteousness really is. The judgement of the Prince
of this world is indeed an instance of that divine
judgement of whose reality our moral torpor suggests
doubt, and as we reflect upon it we can stimulate our
own anticipation of that judgement to the quickening
of our sluggish consciences. This would be much;
but it is the lesser part of what the words of the Lord
convey.

He will convict the world: He will prove the world
wrong — and us with the world so far as we share
the outlook of the world — *in respect of sin, and of
righteousness, and of judgement.* The world has to learn
that its very conception of these things is all wrong.
If it tries to avoid sin or to seek righteousness, it does
not avoid or seek the right things ; if it fears or prepares for judgement, it does not fear or prepare for the
right thing.

Of sin, in that they believe not on me. Their unbelief is, so to speak, brought into court, not merely as
evidence that they are sinful, but as proof that they
are wrong in their idea of sin.

We tend to think of sin as consisting of acts which
are done in defiance of conscience or are, whether we
know it or not, contrary to God's command. Some
people even say that so long as a man follows his
conscience he cannot be committing sin. (The theo-
logian would say that he is certainly not committing
" formal sin " but he may be committing " material
sin ".) Certainly a man should follow his conscience;
but that is not the whole of his duty. Still more
important is it to enlighten conscience itself, lest
" the light that is in us be darkness " (*St. Matthew* vi,
23). The greatest crimes in history have been per-
petrated at the bidding of conscience — such as the
Spanish Inquisition. The disciples were warned to
expect a time when *whosoever killeth you will think*

G

that he is offering worship to God (2). A sin committed
against the light is more wicked than another; the
man who does it is more guilty. But sin is something
much wider and deeper than guilt. Everything
which is other than God would have it be is sin.
" All have sinned and fall short of the glory of God "
(*Romans* iii, 23); that is the definition of sin—to fall
short of the glory of God! It is not enough that
we should be as good as the people about us; nothing
is enough except that we should be as good as God —
" Ye therefore shall be perfect as your heavenly Father
is perfect " (*St. Matthew* v, 48). But we shall not set
ourselves that standard, to say nothing of attaining
it, if we are left to our own resources. And we do not
know what the perfection of God is until we have
seen it in Christ. Unless we *believe on* Him we are
bound to be wrong in our whole idea about sin; for
apart from that faith we have neither the stimulus nor
the capacity to frame the true standard.

So the world's failure to believe on Christ is the
proof that the world is wrong in its conception of what
sin is. Here the world is likely to protest. " A man
cannot help his beliefs ", they say; " he is responsible
for acting up to them but he is not answerable for
what does or does not seem to be true." Is that so?
When a proposition is made to a man, he exercises
his judgement to the best of his ability; but is that
" best " as good as it might have been? If it is lacking in some sensitiveness which a more careful discipline of mind would have supplied, he is responsible
for his error even though he did his best at the
moment. This principle is both clearer and more
important in proportion as the matter presented concerns more intimately our moral and spiritual life.
A high ideal may be presented to a man and he con-
siders whether or not he shall accept it for the guidance
of his life. His answer must depend on his character.
He may give the truest and wisest answer of which he

is then capable; but if he has allowed himself to settle
down to a selfish outlook or to materialist standards,
this will affect his judgement. He will reject the ideal
in perfect sincerity; but that sincerity is not so much
a justification of his conduct as a measure of his sin.

So, supremely, the divine revelation in Christ
operates in judgement upon those to whom it is
offered (iii, 19). Can men see in the perfect self-
sacrifice of Christ the power and wisdom of God? If
so, they are in the way of salvation; if not, they are on
the way of perdition. " The word of the Cross is
to them that are perishing foolishness; but unto us
which are being saved it is the power of God. . . . We
proclaim a Messiah on a cross, to Jews a scandal and
to Gentiles an absurdity, but to those who are called,
a Messiah who is God's power and God's wisdom "
(*I Corinthians* i, 18, 23, 24).

If then we fail to commit ourselves in trust to
Christ when His revelation is before us, it proves not
only that we are sinful, but that we are wrong in our
conception of sin. For if only we could realise that,
inasmuch as God is Love, the essence of sin is love's
opposite, that is to say, self-centredness, our understanding of this would impel us to cast ourselves upon
the divine love which alone can win us from our
evil state. We are not impelled to that trust, because
we wrongly diagnose our disease. We try to cure our
symptoms — our habits of lying, or cheating, or
resentment, or envy, or contempt, or impurity — but
we leave the disease itself alone. But the disease is
that we are self-centred, not God-centred; the cure
for that is faith; if we do not at least seek after faith,
it proves that we have not understood the nature of
our trouble: if we knew our sickness, we should know
our need of the physician.

*Of righteousness, in that to the Father I go my way
and no longer do ye take note of me.* The world's notion
of righteousness is wrong in the same way as its

notion of sin. The world admires and approves its honourable and successful men; and that is right enough. But real sacrifice for higher than material or patriotic causes it regards with anxiety and alarm. Even if we can conceive that for ourselves such sacrifice would be righteous, we show how little its claim has gripped us when we recall how we shrink from commending that same claim to our neighbours. We do not believe in any radical self-sacrifice enough to recommend it to our friends, even when we might follow that course ourselves. And when the course in question involves defiance of the State, and the disgrace of imprisonment or a criminal's execution, we regard it as fanatical.

The Lord was about to suffer that disgrace. In the eyes of the worldly-wise He was behaving foolishly; He was cutting short a career of great usefulness, which He could easily have continued; His attitude was quixotic. So an observer by no means cynical might say. But that observer and the world represented by him would be missing the real truth of the situation. The appearance of a criminal's execution and of the untimely collapse of His cause is superficial only: the reality is that *to the Father I go my way and no longer do ye take note of me*.

To the Father I go my way: this is the order of words in the original. Not to the felon's grave, but *to the Father*; not under compulsion of force, but *I go my way*. This complete abandonment to the will of God is the real righteousness, and its issue is not the misery of humiliation but " the joy that was set before Him " (*Hebrews* xii, 2).

No longer do ye take note of me: the word translated *take note of* is that which is used of the people taking note of the miracles (vi, 2) and of the believer taking no note of death (viii, 51). It is used of physical as distinguished from spiritual vision; in verses 16-19 the contrast is emphatic; and it is used of such

physical " seeing " as involves attention. While the
Lord was with them in the flesh, of course the disciples watched and took note of His every word and
action.   It might easily seem that they depended
entirely on His outward presence among them.   " If
He be removed ", the world might well say, " His
cause will collapse ".   But it is part of the proof of
righteousness in that Life which the world condemned,
that disciples, who can take note of Him no longer,
are disciples still.   The Spirit, pointing out that what
the world thought death and failure is really victory
and fulfilment, and that a discipleship which began
as external companionship should persist as spiritual
agency, exhibits the true nature of righteousness —
not the punctual fulfilment of contracts (though that
also is righteous) but total self-commitment to the
righteous Father (xvii, 25).

*Of judgement in that the prince of this world hath
been judged.*   If men's conception of sin and of righteousness needs to be deepened, quite equally is this
true of their thought of judgement. We tend to think
of the Divine Judgement as being the infliction upon
us by an irresistible Despot of penalties, not growing
out of our characters and deeds, but imposed from
without.   All through this Gospel we have been
learning that this is not the true account of Judgement;
see especially iii, 19 and the passages collected in the
comment upon it.   The Divine Judgement is the
verdict upon us which consists in our reaction to *the
light* (iii, 19) when it is offered to us; by that reaction
we are stamped as *sons of light* (xii, 36) or as children
of darkness.   If we *love the darkness rather than the
light* (iii, 19) there is nothing more or worse to be
done to us. With Judas we go out from the Light of
the world into the night (xiii, 30).

The world thought that it was judging Christ
when Caiaphas rent his clothes, and the people shouted
" He is worthy of death ", and Pilate gave sentence

as they desired. But we know that it was they, and not He, upon whom sentence was then passed. History has vindicated His claim that in rejecting Him the Prince of this world was already judged. The Spirit points to this reversal and by means of it teaches us how wrong our own idea of judgement is.

How dread a Companion and Guide, then, is this Comforter! We are distressed about some special fault, and ask His aid to overcome it; whereupon He tells us that our real trouble is our self-complacence and self-reliance, and if it is His help that we seek, He will rouse us from these. But we do not want that at all! Indeed our chief reason for wanting to overcome that special fault was that it disturbed our self-complacence, which we hoped, after a little moral effort, to enjoy once more. Or we seek His aid in living according to our standard of righteousness and are told that this standard is hardly worth striving after: only the total committal of "ourselves, our souls and bodies, to be a reasonable, holy and lively sacrifice" is real righteousness. Or we turn to Him to be our Paraclete, our Advocate, in the judgement; and He tells us that we are judged already by our steady preference of our way to God's.

When we pray "Come, Holy Ghost, our souls inspire", we had better know what we are about. He will not carry us to easy triumphs and gratifying successes; more probably He will set us to some task for God in the full intention that we shall fail, so that others, learning wisdom by our failure, may carry the good cause forward. He may take us through loneliness, desertion by friends, apparent desertion even by God; that was the way Christ went to the Father. He may drive us into the wilderness to be tempted of the devil. He may lead us from the Mount of Transfiguration (if He ever lets us climb it) to the hill that is called the Place of a Skull. For if we invoke Him, it must be to help us in doing God's will, not ours.   We cannot call upon the

> Creator Spirit, by whose aid
> The world's foundations first were laid

in order to use omnipotence for the supply of our futile pleasures or the success of our futile plans.   If we invoke Him, we must be ready for the glorious pain of being caught by His power out of our petty orbit into the eternal purposes of the Almighty, in whose onward sweep our lives are as a speck of dust. The soul that is filled with the Spirit must have become purged of all pride or love of ease, all self-complacence and self-reliance; but that soul has found the only real dignity, the only lasting joy. Come then, Great Spirit, come.   Convict the world; and convict my timid soul.

*

(3) The Comforter and the Disciples

12-15. Yet many things have I to say to you, but ye cannot bear them now.   But when He is come, the Spirit of truth, he will guide you into truth in its entirety.   For he will not speak from himself, but as many things as he shall hear he will speak, and the things that are coming he will declare to you.   He will glorify me, because from out what is mine he will take and will declare to you. All things as many as the Father hath are mine; that is why I said that from out what is mine he will take and will declare to you.

Yet many things have I to say to you, but ye cannot bear them now.   What teaching can be given depends on the pupil's capacity to receive.   Every schoolmaster has had his old pupils come back, perhaps from the University, and say what a difference it has made to them that someone has told them this or that; " but why " one of them adds " did no one tell us that before? "   The schoolmaster remembers, but wisely does not say, that he did tell them, many times.   But they could not bear it then; they were not ready;

and the words passed by them. So the Lord knows that His disciples could not receive much that He would tell them. They have not yet the strength to accept and carry it: *ye cannot bear them now*. Just as they could not *follow Him now* but should *follow afterwards* (xiii, 36) on His spiritual pilgrimage, so their minds cannot yet enter into the full meaning of His ministry and His passion, but shall be led to this later by the Spirit.

It is no true loyalty to the mind of the Lord which confines attention to what He did and said on earth. Then He kept His teaching within the range of His disciples' apprehension. Even so they would not grasp all His meaning; but they would grasp enough to start on the mental pilgrimage or exploration, on which they should be carried further by the Spirit. We are most loyal to the mind of Christ when we are most receptive of all that the Apostles, under the guidance of the Spirit, learnt and taught, and of all that the same Spirit would teach us now.

But when He is come: here, as again in the saying *He will glorify me*, the word *He* is emphatic. To say " that one " every time is unnatural and intolerably clumsy. But the stress is on the word *He*, not on the word *come*. It is not the future date to which the disciples are pointed so much as to the Agent of their illumination.

The Spirit of truth, He will guide you into truth in its entirety. The title is repeated from xv, 26, where also the function associated with it is witness to Jesus Himself. *The Spirit of truth will guide you into truth in its entirety*. If we say " Spirit of truth " we must say " into truth "; if we say " into the truth " or " into all the truth " we must say " Spirit of the truth "; for the phrases are identical and balance each other. There is, of course, no reference intended to the discovery of scientific or general historical truth; though, inasmuch as all truth of every kind must ultimately be one, that thought is not at all alien from what is intended. The immediate reference is to the understanding of the Lord Jesus; since He is the Word of God, this will supply the clue to the understanding of all else, but that comes by way of corollary. The Holy Spirit is the Spirit of truth because He leads men to an ever fuller understanding of Jesus Who is *the truth* (xiv, 6), till at last we apprehend it *in its entirety* or as a whole.

He will not speak from Himself any more than the Lord had done (vii, 17); both the Lord and the Spirit speak what they hear from the Father (xv, 15).

The things that are coming — the Passion, Resurrection and Ascension of the Lord — *he will declare to you*. These were more particularly the things that the Lord could not now expound. The events themselves must take place, and then, in the illumination inaugurated at Pentecost, the Apostles would be able to *bear* their message. So it proved; and the Apostolic teaching, given in the power of the Spirit, mainly concerns the themes which, when the Lord spoke, were *the things that are coming*. Let us consider some of them. " Him who knew no sin, he made to be sin on our behalf, that we might become the righteousness of God in Him " (*II Corinthians* v, 21). " Being justified freely by his grace through the redemption that is in Christ Jesus, whom God set forth in his blood — a mercy-seat through faith — to shew his righteousness " (*Romans* iii, 25).[1] " We were buried

---

[1] I am persuaded that ἱλαστήριον here means Mercy Seat, as it does in the LXX — e.g. *Exodus* xxv, 18. The Mercy Seat was sprinkled with the blood of the victim. So God set forth Christ on the Cross in His Blood to be through faith the true Mercy Seat — the place where God's forgiveness meets man's sin. This it can do freely because in the same place, the Cross, is displayed the cost of sin to God, so that forgiveness is possible without any suggestion that God makes light of sin. Thus if we start from the thought of righteousness, the Cross makes forgiveness morally possible; if we start from the thought of forgiveness, the Cross is found " to shew His righteousness ". It is itself the reconciliation of justice and forgiveness.

therefore with him through baptism into death: that like as Christ was raised from the dead through the glory of the Father, so we might also walk in newness of life " (*Romans* vi, 4). " God being rich in mercy, for his great love wherewith he loved us, even when we were dead through our trespasses, quickened us together with Christ (by grace have ye been saved) and raised us up with him and made us to sit with him in the heavenly places in Christ Jesus " (*Ephesians* ii, 6). " Having therefore, brethren, boldness to enter into the holy place by the blood of Jesus, by the way which he dedicated for us, a new and living way, through the veil, that is to say his flesh " (*Hebrews* x, 19, 20). These are some of the declarations made by the Spirit to the Apostles and through them to us concerning the things which, when the Lord spoke, were *coming*. How could the disciples *bear them* then? There must be, first the events themselves; then the new illumination ; then the experience of that " fellowship " in the Spirit which led the disciples to a consciousness of union with one another in the Lord and so made clear what was their true relationship to Him (though He gave its principle in the figure of the Vine) and, by consequence, what His Death, Resurrection and Ascension meant to them.

These *things that are coming* concern the Lord. *He will glorify me* as He makes clear the meaning of what the Lord had spoken and done. Christ is glorified in the Passion (xii, 23, 24; xiii, 31-33; xvii, 1). That glorification is the necessary condition which must be fulfilled before the Spirit can come (vii, 39; xvi, 7). When the Spirit comes He completes that glorification by making its full meaning clear to those who receive Him.

For what the Spirit does is not to impart knowledge of other themes or future events but to interpret Christ. *He from out what is mine will take and will declare to you*. Yet this does not involve any limita-

tion of His activity as revealer.   For Christ is the
Word *through whose agency all things came to be* (i, 3),
so that to declare Him is to declare the principle of
all things.   Here the same truth is expressed from the
other side.   *All things as many as the Father hath are
mine* so that to say *what is mine* and " what is the
Father's " is to say the same thing.   In the same way
the Lord said that to snatch His own from His hand
or from the Father's hand was the same thing (x, 28,
29).   Because He and the Father are One, the relation
of the Spirit to Him and to the Father is the same.

Each of the last three clauses ends with the refrain
he will declare to you.   The disciple is not to clamour
for the solution of perplexities or for intellectual
mastery of divine mysteries.   What knowledge he has
in this realm is his because the Spirit has declared it
to him; and for the Spirit's declaration he must wait.

*

(4) Sorrow turned to Joy

16-22.   " A little while and ye no longer take note of me and again a
little while and ye will see me."   Some of his disciples therefore
said to one another, " What is this which he saith to us, ' A little
while and ye do not take note of me and a little while and ye will
see me ' and ' Because I go my way to the Father ' ".   So they were
saying, " What is this that he saith, this ' little while '?   We do not
know what he speaketh."   Jesus recognised that they were wishing
to ask him, and said to them, " Concerning this do ye enquire
among themselves, that I said ' A little while and ye do not take
note of me and again a little while and ye will see me '?   Amen,
Amen, I say to you that weep and lament will ye, but the world
will rejoice; ye will be sorrowful, but your sorrow will turn into
joy.   A woman, when she is in travail, hath sorrow, because her
hour is come.   But when the child is born, she is no longer mindful
of the anguish for the joy that there is born a man into the world.
And ye therefore now have sorrow; but I shall see you again and
your heart will rejoice, and your joy no man taketh from you."

The rather elaborately full record of this conversation reflects the concern of the Church for

which the Gospel was written. The delay of Christ's
" return " was a cause of serious perplexity. How
were devout Christians to answer the " mockers "
who said, " Where is the promise of his coming? for,
from the day that the fathers fell asleep, all things
continue as they were from the beginning of the
creation " (*II Peter* iii, 4). The Lord had spoken of
His Coming as imminent; there was no doubt about
that. Was He deluded?

No; He was misunderstood. The Coming is
the Cross and the ingathering of its triumph through
the Resurrection, Ascension, Pentecost, the Evangelisation of the World, and the final Consummation;
its focal moment is the Cross and Resurrection. So
He assured the High Priest at His trial that from
that moment Daniel's prophecy was fulfilled (*St.
Matthew* xxvi, 64; *St. Luke* xxii, 69). Certainly it
was imminent. But this transformation of the meaning
of the Coming was too great for their apprehension.
To explain it in advance was impossible. The event
itself was necessary to generate the experience by which
alone it could be apprehended. So words were spoken
which provided the clue to the mystery though at this
stage they could scarcely do more than darken it.
Later, remembered in the light of both event and
experience, they would be seen to have offered a preparation, and to shew that the Lord's own expectation, far from being frustrated, had been precisely
fulfilled.[1] He had spoken of *a little while* and at the
time it had puzzled the disciples. Now, when the
Evangelist is writing, they can look back and realise
that all has been as He foresaw.

A little while and ye no longer take note of me. The
translation is clumsy; perhaps the Revised Version
" behold me no more " should be retained; but the
word used seemed to call for the translation chosen

[1] On the subject of our Lord's thought of the Coming, see Introduction,
pp. xxx and xxxi.

or something very similar on some previous occasions, especially vi, 2 and viii, 51; in any case it is sharply contrasted with " see " in the following phrase. The Authorised Version makes the passage far more obscure by using " see " in both places.

While the Lord was with them, the disciples noted all that He said and did. Now the opportunity for that is drawing to an end. From the moment of His death they can " behold " or take note of Him no longer.

And again a little while and ye will see me. After a short interval of desolation, they will *see* Him with the direct spiritual vision which brings full personal knowledge and communion: this would begin at once after the Resurrection, when the new era of the Son of Man would be inaugurated.

Some of the disciples murmur the phrase to one another, and connect with it another which He has used and which was hard to grasp clearly — *because I go my way to the Father,* which had before been connected with these words *no longer do ye take note of me* (10). They can only confess themselves baffled. The Lord recognises their perplexity; He repeats the mysterious phrases once again; and then He sketches the experience that awaits them in another way.

Weep and lament will ye, but the world shall rejoice. For two days they will mourn a lost Leader and Friend, while the world rejoices that it is rid of a trouble-maker.

Ye will be sorrowful, but your sorrow will turn into joy. It is not only that joy will take the place of sorrow, but the sorrow itself becomes the joy. The Cross is not for Christians a stumbling-block which the Resurrection has removed; it is not a defeat of which the effect has been cancelled by a subsequent victory. It is itself the triumph. What was the devil's worst is become God's best. He has " Led captivity captive " (*Ephesians* iv, 8 quoting *Psalm* lviii, 18). Sorrow is become joy. The Christian joy and hope do not arise from an ignoring of the evil in the world, but from facing it at its worst. The light that shines for ever in the Church breaks out of the veriest pit of gloom.

Ye therefore now have sorrow. The Christian is no Stoic. He does not refuse the sorrow occasioned by the mortal lot of man and (still more bitterly) by his sin. He accepts and bears it. But he bears it "in sure and certain hope".

But I shall see you again, and your heart will rejoice, and your joy no one taketh from you. The joy of Easter once truly experienced becomes a pervading atmosphere which the soul thenceforth breathes for ever. "Who shall separate us from the love of Christ? shall tribulation or anguish or persecution or famine or nakedness or peril or sword? Even as it is written, ' For thy sake we are killed all the day long; we were accounted as sheep for the slaughter '. Nay, in all these things we are more than conquerors through him that loved us. For I am persuaded that neither death, nor life, nor angels, nor principalities, nor things present, nor things to come, nor powers, nor height, nor depth, nor any other creature, shall be able to separate us from the love of God, which is in Christ Jesus our Lord" (*Romans* viii, 35-39). St. Paul's glorious outburst reflecting his own experience is no more than a symphony on the theme propounded before the event by the Lord Himself.

*

(5) PRAYER AND ITS ANSWER

23-27. "And in that day ye will ask me no question. Amen, Amen, I say to you, if ye pray anything of the Father, he will give it you, in my name. Until now ye did not pray anything in my name; pray, and ye will receive, that your joy may be fulfilled. These things in parables have I spoken to you; an hour cometh when no longer in parables shall I speak to you, but in open speech shall bring you news of the Father. In that day, in my name will ye

pray and I say not to you that I will ask the Father concerning you;
for the Father himself loveth you because ye have loved me and
have believed that I came forth from the presence of God."

The changes in the word for " ask " are exaggerated
by any English translation which notices them at all;
but the feeling tone of the words is not quite the same.
Petitions and enquiries overlap in certain ways.   The
opening phrase in this passage suggests a deference
which is absent from the later phrases until the first
recurs in a new context.   The disciples are not here
thought of as making petitions to their Lord, but rather
as consulting Him and awaiting His decision.   This
is our proper attitude in prayer, and it is noteworthy
that it recurs in 26 of the attitude of the Son to the
Father, so that even in prayer the analogy still holds
— We : Christ : : Christ : the Father; though evidently in the latter case there is no absence in the Son
of full knowledge concerning the Father's mind.

But a new principle of prayer has been laid down —
Prayer which is offered and granted *in my name*.   This
principle was stated in xiv. 13 and again in xv, 16.
Here there is an addition to the thought then expressed; for the crucial words *in my name* are, so to
speak, held back, so as to be connected with *he will
give it you* as well as with *if ye pray anything*.   Both the
prayer and its answer are in His Name.   We have
already seen what is meant for us by prayer in the
Name of Christ (xv, 16); it means that we pray as His
representatives, as He would pray in our place, as
He does pray in heaven.   But we are at first surprised
at the thought that the Father gives in His Name the
answer to our prayer; yet we have already been told
(xiv, 26) that the Father sends the Spirit in the Name
of the Son.   For in fact the Son is the Mediator,
through whom our prayers ascend to the Father and
through whom the Father's love descends in bless-
ings on His children.   This does not interpose a
barrier between God and Man, for the Mediator is

Himself both God and Man. Another way of approaching this thought would be to say that through the union of divine and human in Jesus Christ, we have both more assured access to the Father (*Ephesians* ii, 18 and iii, 12) and more abundant blessing from the Father. It is the same thought which is also expressed in i, 51, where the Lord speaks of *the angels of God ascending and descending upon the Son of Man*.

It is a new experience of worship that is offered. *Until now ye did not pray anything in my name.* They were men of prayer; but they had prayed as devout Jews, not as disciples checking each desire as it suggested itself for presentation to the Father by reference to the Mind of their Master. That is the prayer that will always be answered, and answered with the consequence of a joy that is complete; *pray* (*sc.* in my name) *and ye will receive, that your joy may be fulfilled.*

All this will be the experience of the disciples *in that day* — the day when the Lord sees them again, bestowing the joy that no one can take from them, the day of His Easter greeting and His threefold Easter gift of peace, of mission, and of holy spirit. That day is now very near; its fuller revelation is at hand. *These things in parables have I spoken to you; an hour cometh when no longer in parables shall I speak to you, but in open speech shall bring you news of the Father.* The revelation through the Spirit which would follow the Resurrection would be clearer than it was possible to give at the earlier time when *Jesus was not yet glorified* (vii, 39). And this clearer revelation can be ours now, if we are willing to " abide in Him and His words abide in us " (xv, 7).

In that day (which is now equivalent to saying " in the power of the Spirit whom I will send "), *in my name ye will pray, and I say not to you that I will ask the Father concerning you :* once again the word for

asking questions is substituted for that which stands
for making petitions, as though the Son would not
presume to ask outright for any boon, but might
consult the Father concerning what His loving wisdom
would decide; and even that will be unnecessary *for
the Father himself loveth you, because ye have loved me
and have believed that I came forth from the presence of
God.* The word for *loveth* and *loved* is not that which
represents the universal and self-giving love of God,
but that which represents friendship; perhaps we may
translate thus: *the Father himself is friendly to you
because ye have been my friends.* Within that holy
love of God which goes forth to all men — *So God
loved the world* (iii, 16) — there is room for particular
relationships to individual men and women, and those
whose hearts are won to affection for the Lord Jesus
are thereby brought into a special relation of tender
intimacy with the Father. An earthly father who loves
all his children equally may yet have special ties of
intimacy with each one, a peculiar tenderness in every
case; this one is so eager, that one so gentle, another
so wistfully affectionate; he does not love one more
than another, but he loves each differently. It makes
the love of God seem less remote in its holiness when
we learn that it contains within itself a similar varia-
tion of individual attachment. Nor need any be
excluded from the " friendship " of God that is here
spoken of, for all may be " friends " of Jesus.

Yet it is not a mere human friendship that so
qualifies the disciples; it is this in combination with
the faith which recognises His mission: *ye have
believed that I came forth from the presence of God* — not
only *from God* (30) as a messenger might come whom
God had summoned to receive instructions and then
despatched, but one who dwelt ever with God and
was sent forth from the divine presence which was
His home.

*

H

(6) THE DIVINE TRIUMPH

28-33. " I came forth from the Father and am come into the world; again, I leave the world and depart to the Father." His disciples say, " Lo, now in open speech thou speakest and sayest no parable; now we know that thou knowest all things and hast not need that any one should ask thee. By this we believe that thou camest forth from God." Jesus answered them, " At this moment ye believe. Behold, there cometh an hour, and it is come, that ye will be scattered each to his own home, and me ye will leave alone, and yet I am not alone because the Father is with me. These things have I spoken to you that in me ye may have peace. In the world ye have tribulation; but be of good cheer, I have overcome the world."

The reference to the faith of the disciples (27) leads to this apparently clear declaration. *I came forth from the Father and am come into the world; again, I leave the world and depart to the Father.* The preposition in the phrase *from the Father* very nearly means *out of the Father*; it would be a mistake to press it, but the suggestion of an intimate identity with the Father before the Incarnation is conveyed. The disciples seem to think that this is the declaration in open speech which had been promised. But is it really so clear what is meant by " coming into the world " where the words are used of Him through whom all things came to be (i, 3), or what is meant by " departure to the Father " when spoken of Him who is always in the bosom of the Father (i, 18; see 32). In fact the disciples shew, by a slight but significant misquotation, that, though in one sense they believe, yet their understanding is very limited. They welcome the plainness of language: *Now in open speech thou speakest and sayest no parable. Now we know that thou knowest all things* (even our unspoken thoughts) *and needest not that any man should ask thee.* The Lord had read their longing for a clear declaration, and had given it though they had not asked and the longing was unexpressed. *By this we believe that thou camest forth from God.*   A sincere affirmation of a true faith. And yet Nicodemus had said just the same! (iii, 2). For though the Lord had said that He came *from the presence of* or *from beside God* (παρά, 27) and *out of God* (ἐκ, 28), the disciples confess no more than that He came *from God* (ἀπό, 30) as a mere messenger might come.   It is something to believe that; but it is very far short of the faith for which the Lord had asked: *Believe me that I am in the Father and the Father in me; In that day ye shall recognise that I am in the Father, and ye in me, and I in you* (xiv, 11, 20).

We should not, then, be surprised that the Lord accepts this profession of faith as no more than a very incomplete instalment.   It will not survive the shock that awaits it.   *At this moment ye believe:* yes, in the inspiration of what had happened in the Upper Room and of the wonderful awe-creating words, they do for the time and in a measure believe.   But it will not last.   *Behold, there cometh an hour, and it is come, that ye will be scattered each to his own home.*   The prophecy of Zechariah xiii, 7 — " Smite the shepherd and the sheep shall be scattered " — was prominent in the mind of the Lord that night (*St. Mark* xiv, 27).   And it was fulfilled — " they all left him and fled " (*St. Mark* xiv, 50).   *And me ye will leave alone.*   He went forth alone bearing His cross, no follower attending on Him.   He alone was then the true Israel, the Servant of the Lord, the Vine of God — utterly deserted, utterly alone.

Yet this was not the deepest truth; it would seem so to others; it would seem so to Himself (*St. Mark* xv, 34); but in deepest truth it would not be so; and as He looks forward to what awaits Him He knows the truth: *and yet I am not alone because the Father is with me.*   At every stage of His " departure to the Father " the Father is with Him, even as at every stage of our pilgrimage to the Father's home we are at home with the Father (xiv, 2).

These things have I spoken to you — the last of the seven iterations of this phrase (xiv, 25; xv, 11; xvi, 1, 6, 25, 33) as the great discourse reaches its conclusion, *that in me ye may have peace.* Peace, *the peace that is mine*, was the promise that accompanied the first mention of the Comforter (xiv, 26, 27); so now it is the last promised gift. Peace — the greatest need of the world and of the soul: *in me ye may have peace.* Only in Him; not in the world, till the world takes Him for its Lord. *In the world ye have tribulation;* that remains true; and the tribulation will become more grievous rather than less (xvi, 1-4). But those who are in Him will not heed it. *Be of good cheer; I have overcome the world.*

That those words should be spoken then is a fact that almost paralyses feeling, even the feelings of awe and adoration. He knew what was before Him; yet He can say *I have overcome the world.* For what the world thought His shame was His glory and what the world thought His defeat was His victory. "Having put off from himself his body, he made a show of the principalities and powers openly, triumphing over them in the Cross" (*Colossians* ii, 15). Not in gloom or depression, but in solemn triumph, "for the joy that was set before him" (*Hebrews* xii, 2), He moves forward to His death. Soon the crown of glory and thorns will be upon His brow; soon upon His gallows-throne He will be *lifted up*; already He is the conqueror; *I have overcome the world.*

APPENDIX

THE LORD'S TEACHING ON PRAYER

In Chapter XVI we find the culmination of the Lord's teaching on Prayer; in Chapter XVII we have

His own prayer of self-consecration offered as Priest-Victim, Victim-Priest. It is worth while to pause for a moment and consider His teaching on Prayer as a whole.

First must be put the fundamental principle that God is perfect love and wisdom; He has no need that we should tell Him of our wants or desires; He knows what is for our good better than we do ourselves, and it is always His will to give it: " Your Father knoweth what things ye have need of before ye ask Him " (*St. Matthew* vi, 8). Consequently we must not in prayer have any thought of suggesting to God what was not already in His mind — still less of changing His mind or purpose.

But what things are good for us may depend on our spiritual state. Food which is wholesome and nourishing for those who are in good health may be lethal poison to any who are in high fever. The worst of all diseases of the soul is detachment from God, whether by ignorance or by neglect. If all our wants are supplied while we have no thought of God, this may confirm us in our detachment from Him, and so the things that should have been for our wealth are unto us an occasion of falling (*Psalm* lxix, 22). Consequently the question whether what is normally a blessing, such as deliverance from the enticement of some temptation, will be in actual fact a blessing to me may often depend on whether or not I recognise God as the source of all good things. So the first requirement in prayer is that we trust to God for all blessing.

Our Lord, according to His custom, states this in its place without qualification and without reserve. He goes to the greatest possible length in the demand that as we pray we shall believe that God will hear and answer, and in the promise that God will then grant our petitions. Many sayings might be quoted; one is sufficient: " All things whatsoever ye pray and ask for, believe that ye have received them and ye shall have them " (*St. Mark* xi, 24).

The next requirement is apparently inconsistent with this; for this next requirement is that we should persevere in prayer in spite of disappointment. We are to be sure that God will grant our prayers; and when He does not, we are to go on praying. Our Lord gives His teaching about perseverance in two parables which belong to that well-marked group of parables whose point is that the comparison fails. For in these the Lord illustrates God's dealing with us, or our duty before God, by reference to human actions which are not morally admirable. Such are, evidently, the parable of the Unjust Steward (*St. Luke* xvi, 1-9) and, as I think, the parable of the Labourers in the Vineyard (*St. Matthew* xx, 1-16). The duty of perseverance in prayer is urged upon us in the parables of the Importunate Friend (*St. Luke* xi, 5-10) and of the Unjust Judge (*St. Luke* xviii, 1-8). We know that God does not grant petitions in order to rid Himself of the nuisance which we become by our persistence; His choice of a parallel so completely inapposite is a challenge to us to seek the real reason why God may make long delay and then grant our request.

The first requirement was perfect confidence. Does God wish to test our confidence? Of course not; He knows perfectly well what it is worth. But He may very likely wish to deepen it. The faith which takes the form — almost necessary at first — of confidence that God will do what we ask, is after all faith in our own judgement as much as faith in God. We may not pray for anything except so far as we believe it to be God's will; that belief is very fallible. The purpose of God's delay may well be to detach our faith in Him from all trust in our own judgement. Scarcely anything deepens and purifies faith in God for His own sake as surely as perseverance in prayer despite long disappointment.

So the purification of confidence by perseverance

leads us to the third and deepest requirement. The other two were enjoined upon all His hearers; this was urged upon His more intimate disciples in these closing discourses recorded by St. John. Here are the great sayings:

"Whatsoever ye shall ask in my name, this will I do, that the Father may be glorified in the Son. If ye shall ask anything in my name, I will do it" (xiv, 13, 14).

"If ye abide in me and my sayings abide in you, ask whatsoever ye will and it shall come to pass for you" (xv, 7).

"If ye ask anything of the Father, he will give it you, in my name; until now ye did not ask anything in my name; ask, and ye will receive, that your joy may be fulfilled" (xvi, 23, 24).

When the condition mentioned is satisfied, our wills are identified with the will of God; we are then praying for what He desires to give and waits to give until we recognise Him as its source so that our reception of it will strengthen our faith and not encourage our neglect of Him.

This means that the essential act of prayer is not the bending of God's will to ours — of course not — but the bending of our wills to His. The proper outline of a Christian's prayer is not "Please do for me what I want" but "Please do in me, with me and through me what you want". The pattern prayer that our Lord taught us is based on this principle; "after this manner pray ye" (*St. Matthew* vi, 9). What is the manner?

When we come into our Father's presence, our Lord seems to say, we should be so filled with the thought of Him that we forget all about ourselves, our hopes, our needs, even our sins; what we want most of all and therefore utter first is that all men may know how glorious God is and reverence Him accordingly — "Hallowed be thy Name". (How often do we pray that? We say it every day; but do we pray it?) Our next desire is to be that everyone should obey Him, so that He is truly King of His own world — " Thy kingdom come "; then that His whole purpose of love may be carried out, unspoilt by the selfishness in ourselves and others — " Thy will be done ". Only after this do we turn to ourselves, and when we do it is to ask for those things which are necessary if we are to serve God with all our hearts: freedom from harassing anxiety — " daily bread " or " the morrow's bread " ; and restoration to the favour we have forfeited — " forgive us our trespasses " ; and no moral adventures, for there is plenty on the straight path of duty to test character and develop grit without our being " led " to the lairs of dragons — " lead us not into temptation " ; and some evil has a grip upon us from which we cannot free our-selves — " deliver us " from that. And why? Is it because then we shall be good and happy? Not at all. It is because we are all the time concerned with God's Kingdom, Power and Glory.

The two sons of Zebedee once approached the Lord with a prayer which perfectly illustrates the wrong way to pray: " Master, we would that thou shouldst do for us whatsoever we shall ask of thee ". After that, we are not surprised that their request was selfish in the worst sense — it was for something by gaining which they would keep others out of it. To such a prayer for selfish advantage there is and can be only one answer: Can you share My sacrifice? (*St. Mark* x, 35-38).

The essence of prayer is to seek how we may share that sacrifice. It finds its fullest expression in the Eucharist where we offer ourselves to Christ that He may unite us with Himself in His perfect self-offering to the Father — that self-offering to which He dedicated Himself in the great prayer which St. John now calls us to hear with adoring wonder.

CHAPTER XVII

WE now come to what is, perhaps, the most sacred passage even in the four Gospels — the record of the Lord's prayer of self-dedication as it lived in the memory and imagination of His most intimate friend. It consists of three main sections:

(1) The Son and the Father (1-5).
(2) The Son and the disciples (6-19).
(3) The Son, the disciples and the world (20-26).

*

(1) THE SON AND THE FATHER

1-5. These things spake Jesus, and lifting up his eyes to heaven he said, " Father, come is the hour; glorify thy Son that the Son may glorify thee, as thou gavest to him authority over all flesh that all which thou hast given him — he may give to them eternal Life. (And this is the eternal Life, to know thee the only true God, and whom thou sendedst — Jesus Christ.) I glorified thee on the earth by finishing the work which thou hast given me to do. And now glorify thou me, Father, in thine own presence with the glory which I had, before the world was, in thy presence."

These things: the whole discourse from xiii, 31 onwards, but especially its closing words — *I have overcome the world* (xvi, 33). It is in the consciousness of victory and accomplishment (4) that the Lord dedicates Himself to the final sacrifice. So the author of *Hebrews* thinks of Him as going to His death like the victim wearing festal garlands and enduring the Cross in scorn of contempt because He is upheld by " the joy that was set before Him " (*Hebrews* ii, 9 — where see Nairne's commentary [1] — and xii, 2).

[1] *The Epistle of Priesthood,* pp. 308-314, especially 313-314.

These things: the discourse which ended with the declaration *I have overcome the world* or *I have conquered the universe,* had begun with the words *Now was glorified the Son of Man* (xiii, 31) uttered as the door closed behind Judas. Then He had committed Himself to the way of the Cross; now He accepts and welcomes it.

Lifting up his eyes to heaven, he said " Father ": So it had been before the recalling of Lazarus from death to life (xi, 41). So it is now as He enters on His own passage from life to death. Always His trust is in the Father to whom His obedience is given. So it will be at the very close: " Father, into thy hands I commend my spirit " (*St. Luke* xxiii, 46).

" Father, come is the hour; glorify thy Son." When the Greeks came He had greeted their approach with the words: *Come is the hour that the Son of Man may be glorified,* and went on at once to speak of the harvest that can only come through death (xii, 23, 24). When Judas had gone out into the night He said *Now was glorified the Son of Man.* Here is the third use of the solemn phrase: *Come is the hour; glorify thy Son.* It is the hour for the Son of Man to be *lifted up* (xii, 32, 34). His glory is about to reach its full splendour: for it is the glory or shining forth of love, and *greater love than this hath no man, that a man lay down his life on behalf of his friends* (xv, 13).

Glorify thy Son, that the Son may glorify thee. The glory of the Father and that of the Son are inseparable. The Father glorifies the Son by sustaining Him in His perfect obedience even unto death, and the Son glorifies the Father by the perfection of the obedience which He offers. Because God is Love, the Cross is the glory, or, if we will, the " effulgence of the glory " (*Hebrews* i, 3) alike of the Father and of the Son.

The Cross is the glory of God because self-sacrifice is the expression of love. That glory would be complete in itself even if it had no consequences. But in

fact what is revealed in the Cross is not only the perfection of the divine love, but its triumph. For by
its sacrifice the divine love wins those who can appreciate it out of their selfishness which is spiritual death
into loving fellowship with itself which is true life:
" we know that we have passed out of death into Life,
because we love the brethren " (*I John* iii, 14). But
we do not effect that passage in any strength of our
own; it is the gift of God through Christ: *as thou
gavest to him to have authority over all flesh that all
which thou hast given him — he may give to them
eternal Life.*

To the Son is given *authority to execute judgment
because he is Son of Man* (v. 27). So far this might be
displayed in condemnation or in pardon. But if the
Father now perfectly glorifies the Son, and the Son
perfectly glorifies the Father — if, in other words, that
burning love which is the heart of the Godhead be
displayed — then the authority of the Son will be
exercised in the gift of eternal Life. For the Judge
will be Himself the Saviour.

How far this salvation extends is left undefined.
It reaches *all which thou hast given him,* for if any man
responds to the love of God in Christ he does so in
virtue of the Father's act; He had said before, *No man
can come to me except the Father which sent me draw
him* (vi, 44); and those words were at once followed
by the promise — *and I will raise him up at the last
day.* So here the gift of the Son to those whom the
Father has given to Him is *eternal life.* They are
thought of as a single company, a single gift — *that
which thou hast given him.* For in Him we are one; in
so far as we are not one we are not yet in Him; and
the prayer for the disciples which follows is primarily
that they may be one (11). To every member of this
fellowship, given by the Father to the Son, the Son
will give eternal life, if so be that the Father glorify
the Son and the Son the Father.

The condition is indispensable; but if it be fulfilled the consequence is inevitable. For *this is the eternal life, to know thee the only true God, and whom thou sendedst, Jesus Christ.* This knowledge does not earn eternal life; it is eternal life. Do we hesitate to accept that? Does it seem to us that just " knowing " a theological truth cannot be an adequate occupation for eternity? Certainly it could not be. But the word for *know* here is not that which stands for a grasp of truth; it is that which stands for personal acquaintance. Even in human friendships there is the constant delight of new discoveries by each in the character of the other. Eternity cannot be too long for our finite spirits to advance in knowledge of the infinite God.

We constantly miss the spiritual value of the greatest religious phrases by failing to recall their true meaning. At one time I was much troubled that the climax of the *Veni Creator* should be

> Teach us to know the Father, Son,
> And Thee, of Both, to be but One.

It seemed to suggest that the ultimate purpose of the coming of the Holy Spirit was to persuade us of the truth of an orthodox formula. But that is mere thoughtlessness. If a man once knows the Spirit within him, the source of all his aspiration after holiness, as indeed the Spirit of Jesus Christ, and if he knows this Spirit of Jesus Christ within himself as none other than the Spirit of the Eternal and Almighty God, what more can he want? *This is the eternal life.*

This definition of eternal life can hardly be regarded as a part of the prayer addressed by our Lord to the Father. It is a comment inserted by the Evangelist. But his mind is so identified with its content — in this instance the prayer offered by the Lord — that he so phrases his comment as to make it, in grammatical construction, part of the prayer. It is a signal instance of the extent to which his mind and his theme have

interpenetrated one another; this is the cause of modi-
fications in the form of language used, but it is also
the condition of the profound apprehension achieved
and expressed.

*I glorified thee on the earth by finishing the work
which thou hast given me to do.* His active obedience
is the means by which He gives glory to God; so in
Hebrews " Lo, I am come to do thy will, O God "
(*Hebrews* x, 7 quoting *Psalm* xl, 7, 8). He has done
all that can be done *on the earth*. He has loved *to the
uttermost* (xiii, 1) that life in this world permits. One
ultimate perfection of love remains to be achieved, and
He prays that now this may be His — the perfect expression of love in the perfection of self-sacrifice.

*I glorified thee on the earth by finishing the work
which thou hast given me to do.* What work was that?
The revelation of God and, therein, the establishment
of His Kingdom; or, in other words, the living of
a life of perfect love and thereby the winning of that
new control in the hearts of men which is called " holy
spirit ". This He has done so far as it can be done
at all *on earth*, that is, under the conditions of human
life here. And therein He has glorified the Father.
For all that we adore in Him is the Father's glory
shining through Him — *glory as of an only-begotten
from a Father* (i, 14) — and His shewing forth of this
is therefore a giving of glory to the Father.

We are all familiar with this double thought in
other connexions; a boy is trained by his school to a
life of discipline and public service; thereafter the
school is proud of him and honours him; but what
people admire in him is what his school has given to
him, and he, by fidelity to what he has learnt, brings
honour to his school. If we sometimes find this
thought difficult when applied to the highest levels
of spiritual attainment, that is only because of our
disastrous tendency to sheer individualism in things
of the spirit — (see 10 below); it is never possible to

divide up the credit for spiritual achievement and allot portions to different persons.

All that can be done *on earth* — under conditions of earthly life — has been done. But there remains what can be done through death, which is indeed *on earth* so far as it is the close of earthly life, but is already in heaven so far as it is the gateway to fulfilled fellowship with the Father. This it can be, without transition or mediation, only if he who dies is already " made perfect in love " (*I John* iv, 18). That condition has once, and once only, been fulfilled. Because Jesus had *finished the work* of living the life of love, therefore for Him death is immediate passage to the eternal glory. *And now glorify thou me, Father, in thine own presence with the glory which I had before the world was, in thy presence.*

The love that was always perfect according to the existing reality — perfect in the manger, in the home, in the carpenter's shop, in the works of mercy, in the words of life — now reaches its culmination in the absolute self-abnegation of love undimmed — nay, victoriously intensified — by agony and death. This is the perfect fellowship with the Father manifested under the conditions of a sinful world. In one sense it is true to say that the death on the Cross was the gateway to that eternal fellowship and glory ; but more profoundly it is true to say that the death on the Cross is itself the attainment of that fellowship and glory in absolute plenitude.

There is no contradiction between the thought that the Lord Jesus was always, from His Birth, perfectly united with the Father, and saying that He " advanced in favour with God and men " (*St. Luke* ii, 52) or that He " learned obedience by the things which he suffered " (*Hebrews* v, 8). If Herod had succeeded in killing Him in His infancy, there would have been an Incarnation, but no effective revelation of the divine love. He grew as boy and man; at every stage

He was perfect in that stage; only by all the stages of a life matured to full manhood, and then cut short by the self-centredness of a world unable to bear the intolerable glory and judgement of love in its fulness, — only so could the whole revelation be given, the whole power of divine love be exercised, the whole triumph of love over selfishness be won. The Cross is the focus of the eternal glory.

For this perfection of divine love, which had *before the world was* united the Father and the Son, is precisely what sent the Son into the world; *God so loved that he gave* (iii, 16). That love is now to pay the full price and win its longed-for result. It is not the Cross as an isolated episode which is thus the focus of the eternal glory; it is the Cross as the culmination of the life of love, as the achievement of the purpose of the Incarnation, as the projection of divine light across the spaces of the world's darkness. But in fact the Cross is all of these; therefore as He approaches the Cross, and with direct reference to the Cross, the Son prays to the Father, *Now — now glorify thou me, Father, in thine own presence, with the glory which I had, before the world was, in thy presence.*

The Aaronic High Priest entered into the Holiest Place (symbol of the immediate presence of God) to offer the blood of the victim (symbol of the consecrated life of Israel). Our High Priest enters the immediate presence of God in and by the very act of offering His own consecrated life; for to make that offering and to be in that presence are not two things, but one.

In that presence the Lord was *before the world was*; from that presence He has never moved; but, as is necessary in this world of time and change, has *on earth* (4) at once experienced and exhibited its meaning in progressive stages; *now* He will again be in that presence in the uttermost meaning of those words. And He wills that where He is, His disciples also may be with Him (24).

" Having, therefore, brethren, boldness to enter into the holy place, by the blood of Jesus, by the way which he dedicated for us, a new and living way, through the veil, that is to say his flesh; and having a great high priest over the house of God; let us draw near with a true heart in full assurance." " For we have not a high priest that cannot be touched with the feeling of our infirmities; but one that hath been in all points tempted like as we are, apart from (temptations due to past) sin "; " who in the days of his flesh, having offered up prayers and supplications with strong crying and tears unto him that was able to save him out of death, and having been heard for his godly fear, though he was a Son, yet learned obedience by the things which he suffered, and having been made perfect, he became unto all them that obey him the cause of eternal salvation " (*Hebrews* x, 19-22; iv, 15; v, 7-9).

*

(2) The Son and the Disciples (6-19)

6-8. " I manifested thy Name to the men whom thou gavest me out of the world. Thine they were and to me thou gavest them, and thy word they have observed. Now they recognised that all things which thou hast given me are from thee, because the sayings which thou gavest me I have given to them, and they themselves received them, and recognised truly that from thee I came forth and they believed that thou didst send me."

I manifested thy Name. Here, as always, the Name is the revealed Nature. Jesus has manifested the Nature of God. He has not only described it; He has made it apparent; He has exhibited it. But this has not been done to all men, but *to the men whom thou gavest me out of the world.* St. Jude had been perplexed by the thought that the Lord would manifest Himself to the disciples and not to the world (xiv, 22). But in fact nothing else was possible. If God were merely Omnipotence, that could be manifested to everyone by display of miraculous power. But Love cannot be so made manifest; the cynical pride of self-centred men will say that its hope is visionary, its joy tedium, and its sacrifice weakness. How can love so penetrate the shell of the self-complacent as to be recognised by them? So the Lord makes known His Father's Nature of love to those who already belong to the Father as having at least enough of the " image of God " still unobliterated to afford the kinship that makes recognition possible. *Thine they were;* before ever the Lord called them they were truly among the People of God. *And to me thou gavest them;* they heard His call and followed; but this was the Father's doing, for *no man can come to me except the Father which hath sent me draw him* (vi, 44 and 65). *And thy word they have observed;* for the word that the Lord has spoken is what He has heard from His Father (viii, 26, 40; xiv, 24); in observing the teaching of Jesus they were observing the word of the Father.

Now they recognised that all things which thou hast given me are from thee. This is the crucial recognition — not that Jesus is from God, which is the first stage of Christian faith, but that (since this is so) what we find in Him to love and to worship is in truth not His but the Father's. The religious value of the doctrine of the Incarnation is not found in what it affirms concerning the historical Figure, Jesus of Nazareth, but in what it affirms concerning the eternal God. When we know that all the *grace and truth* (i, 14) which shine in Jesus Christ are shining through Him from the Father, we begin to understand who and what God really is.

All this is made possible through the fidelity with which the Son reproduces the mind and activity of the Father (v, 19) — *because the sayings which thou gavest me I have given to them* — and through the faith with which the disciples received that revelation — *and*

I

they themselves received them, and recognised truly that from thee I came forth. Thus the disciples, and we among them, have been led to that principle and activity of Apostleship which is introduced into this prayer by a fivefold refrain (8, 18, 21, 23, 25) — *and they believed that thou didst send me.*

The Apostolic Mission of the Son is the pivot of human history regarded as an arena wherein the divine purpose is being accomplished. All turns on that. From that flows the Apostleship of Church and Ministry. If God sent the Son, then the witness of the Church and its challenge to the world has divine authority. If God sent the Son, then in that act we see disclosed the heart of the Eternal. There is no cause for wonder that in this prayer, offered as His ministry approaches its climax and its close, the Lord should make this a central theme — *that thou didst send me.*

*

9-11. " I ask concerning them. Not concerning the world do I ask, but concerning them whom thou hast given me, because they are thine (and all mine are thine and thine are mine), and I have been glorified in them. And no longer am I in the world, and they are in the world, and I to thee am coming. Holy Father, watch over them in thy Name which thou hast given to me, that they may be one as we."

I ask concerning them. Again, as in xvi, 26, the word used of the Lord's prayer to His Father is that which suggests enquiry rather than petition, as though, not venturing to make request of the Father, He rather consults Him on their behalf. No doubt the version " I pray for them " is right in a translation intended for public or general reading ; but the tone of the word actually used has a suggestion of real beauty and value. Most of our prayers would be the better if they were completely free from any element of clamour or demand, and had more of the quality of a consultation in which we lay the needs of ourselves and of others before our Father that He may supply them as His loving wisdom suggests.

Not concerning the world do I ask. The world is the whole system of nature, including human nature, which " lieth in the evil one " (*I John* v, 19). It was the object of God's redemptive love, which prompted the sending of the Son (iii, 16), and the Lord has overcome it (xvi, 33). It will at last, through the faith of disciples, be won to that same faith (23). But till the disciples are *perfected into one* (23) the world cannot be penetrated by the Gospel. The Lord yearns to redeem it; but He will do this through the continuance of His own apostolic mission in His disciples (18). Therefore His prayer is not directly for the world, but for the disciples, who, after all, are part of the world (15), and through whom the world is to be won.

But concerning them whom thou hast given me, because they are thine. The disciples are a gift of the Father to the Son, for *No man can come to me except the Father which sent me draw him*; *no one can come to me except it have been given to him of my Father* (vi, 44 and 65). The Father could give them because they were His. Indeed between the Father and the Son there is complete identity of ownership; *all mine are thine and thine are mine.* And in these who thus belong both to the Father and the Son the Son has been glorified. The constancy of their loyalty and faith amid all the controversies, even at a time when *many of the disciples went back and walked no more with him* (vi, 66), had brought glory to the Son: *I have been glorified in them.*

And no longer am I in the world. The Lord has been *in the world*, not only locally, but in the sense of sharing all the limitations of human experience alongside His disciples. Now that is ending. Death will at once free Him from the limitations and remove Him from the side of His disciples; but they must remain;

they are in the world; they will still be subject to all
the pressures of the world, including even its hatred
(14), without their Master beside them to steady
their hearts and minds, because separation from them
is involved in the perfecting of His union with the
Father — *I to thee am coming*.

What shall be His prayer for them as He leaves
them to be His witnesses in the world? Shall it be
that they may be courageous? strong? pure in
heart? All these are, no doubt, included in what He
asks, but these are not foremost. Two things He
puts first: that the Father will watch over them with
the protection of His Name — His character revealed in Christ; and that they may be united. *Holy
Father, watch over them in thy Name which thou hast
given to me, that they may be one as we.*

Holy Father. The fundamental element in the con-
cept of holiness is separation from the profane world.
In primitive times this separation is conceived
locally or ceremonially; as faith becomes more spiritual,
the separation is understood as that between righteousness and sin, love and selfishness; but the thought
of separateness persists. Here, where the burden of
the prayer is deliverance from the evil power of the
world (15), the thought of God as wholly separate
from that evil is specially appropriate. The Father is
asked to grant to the disciples His own immunity
from evil.

*Watch over them in thy Name which thou hast given
to me.* The word translated in our versions " keep "
is that which always suggests attentive watching.
The Lord prays His Father to watch in loving care
these disciples to whom the great task is now committed. This He is besought to do in His own Name,
which yet has been given to be the Name of Christ.
Thus St. Paul says that the Father gave to Him " the
name which is above every name " (*Philippians* ii, 9)
and must therefore be God's own Name; if any Name

in the literal sense of that word is in mind, presumably
it is Adonai. But the thought is of revealed character,
not of any spoken sound. This, which is first the
Father's own, the Father has given to the Son. Christ
came " in the Father's name " (v, 43) as representing
Him in the world; but this He could do only because
He was one in character with the Father, so that seeing
Him we see the Father (xiv, 9). In that character of
holy love the Father is prayed to watch over the
disciples, holding them within the sphere of that love,
so that it may possess their hearts — of which the
proof will be their unity among themselves.

That they may be one. The Lord is going away.
In the whole world His cause will be represented by
this little handful of disciples. If they fall apart, the
cause is lost. What is most of all essential is that they
be united. We see in the *Acts of the Apostles* in how
many ways the infant Church was tempted to disunity
— as for example in the doctrinal difference concerning the authority of the Law for Gentile Christians
(*Acts* xv, 1-29) or the personal difference between
Paul and Barnabas concerning John Mark (*Acts* xv,
36-41). Such division at that stage would have been
fatal; it has been sufficiently disastrous coming later,
as it did. So the Lord's prayer was, and (we cannot
doubt) still is, that His disciples may be one.

But the unity of the Church is precious not only
for its utility in strengthening the Church as an
evangelistic agent. It is itself in principle the consummation to which all history moves. The purpose
of God in creation was, and is, to fashion a fellowship
of free spirits knit together by a love in all its members
which answers to the manifested love of God — or,
as St. Paul expresses it, to " sum up all things in
Christ " (*Ephesians* i, 10). The agent of that purpose
is the Church, which is therefore called the Body of
Christ, through the activity and self-edifying of
which Christ Himself is " fulfilled " (*Ephesians* i, 23,

where we should read for "the fulness of him that filleth all in all" — "the fulness of him who, taking things all in all, is being fulfilled". For the fulfilling of Christ to the "measure of the stature of His completeness" (*Ephesians* iv, 13) is the meaning of universal history). The unity of the Church is something much more than unity of ecclesiastical structure, though it cannot be complete without this. It is the love of God in Christ possessing the hearts of men so as to unite them in itself — as the Father and the Son are united in that love of Each for Each which is the Holy Spirit. The unity which the Lord prays that His disciples may enjoy is that which is eternally characteristic of the Tri-une God. It is therefore something much more than a means to any end — even though that end be the evangelisation of the world; it is itself the one worthy end of all human aspiration; it is the life of heaven. For His prayer is not only *that they may be one*; it is *that they may be one as we.*

Before the loftiness of that hope and calling our little experience of unity and fellowship is humbled to the dust. Our friendships, our reconciliations, our unity of spirit in Church gatherings or in missionary conferences — beautiful as they are, and sometimes even wonderful in comparison with our habitual life of sectional rivalries and tensions, yet how poor and petty they appear in the light of the Lord's longing. Let all of us who are concerned in Peace Movements or Faith and Order Movements or "Conversations" with fellow-Christians of other denominations, take note of the judgement under which we stand by virtue of the gulf separating the level of our highest attainment and noblest enterprise, from "the prize of the call upwards which God gives in Christ Jesus" (*Philippians* iii, 14) — *that they may be one as we.*

*

12-13. " When I was with them, I was watching over them in thy
Name which thou hast given to me, and I guarded them, and none
of them was destroyed except the son of destruction, that the
scripture might be fulfilled. But now to thee I am coming; and
these things I speak in the world that they may have the joy that
is mine fulfilled in themselves."

When the Lord was among His disciples He
exercised that loving care which now He prays the
Father to exercise: *When I was with them, I was watch-*
ing over them in thy Name which thou hast given to me.
The divine character of loving wisdom is at once the
motive of His vigilance and the protection in which
He enfolds them. *And I guarded them;* He was, as
it were, their sentry keeping evil influences away from
them. And this was done effectively, for *none of them*
was destroyed except the son of destruction, that the
scripture might be fulfilled. The one exception proves
the rule, for he who was destroyed perished by his
own quality from which no external guardianship
could protect him; he was a *son of destruction.* It was
his nature to destroy; he sought to destroy Jesus,
but he did destroy himself, when *he went immedi-*
ately out, and it was night (xiii, 30). And even therein
was the divine purpose carried towards its accomplishment, as is shewn by the fact that Judas was
fulfilling scripture (see xiii, 18 and the comment
there).

But now to thee I am coming — the first theme of
the prayer and the occasion of all the rest. *And these*
things I speak that they may have the joy that is mine
fulfilled in themselves. The mind and will of the Lord
are in their very nature a prayer to the Father.
There is no need for Him to utter any prayer. But
He does utter it, just as He uttered His thanksgiving
for answer to prayer on another occasion (xi, 41, 42)
in order that His disciples may know what His mind
and will are, and His purpose for them, so that there
may be brought to full measure in them the joy which

is His — the joy of union with the Father and, in Him, with all who are united to Him by faith and love.

*

14-15. " I have given them thy word, and the world hated them, because they are not from the world as I myself am not from the world. I do not ask that thou shouldest take them from the world but that thou shouldest protect them from the evil one."

I have given them thy word. This, repeated in substance from verse 8, is the supreme service of Christ to the disciples. He has given them the self-utterance, the self-disclosure, of the Father. They were able to receive it; the world could not (xiv, 17; 21-24). That is because of the distinctive character of the world and of the disciples; the world hates anything which it cannot understand which yet seems to contain a judgement of itself; so *the world hated them, because they are not from the world as I myself am not from the world.*

The word which I translate *from* throughout this passage is that which I have elsewhere usually translated *out of.* It denotes origin, or character due to origin, or (with words of protection or deliverance) the thought of a hold or grip from which escape is sought.

Thus when it is said that the disciples, even as their Lord, are not from the world, it is origin and character due to origin that are in question. Everything in them which qualified them to receive the Father's word and to become disciples has its origin elsewhere than in this world; but in the passage that follows it is rather separation and protection that are in mind, though the use of the same preposition makes a connecting link.

I do not ask that thou shouldest take them from the world. He is leaving the world, but they must remain in the world, though they do not belong to the world.   They remain there as witnesses, through whom the world itself will at last believe (23).   For all Christians at all times it is a hard question how they are to fulfil their vocation to be in, but not of or from, the world.   The hermit seems to err by going out of the world;   the worldly Christian errs by being of or from the world.   Where is the line of true adjustment between the two?   This is the heart of the controversy on Pacifism.   All that the Lord here lays down is the double principle itself — in the world but not of it.

But that thou shouldest protect them from the evil one.   Here the word translated *protect* is again that which suggests careful attention, translated in verse 11 " Watch over ";   and the word translated *from* suggests that the Evil One has a hold or grip upon them.   They are not snow-white innocents who only need to be kept from all contamination by evil.   We remember the desire of the Sons of Thunder to call down fire from heaven on the Samaritans who would not receive the Lord (*St. Luke* ix, 54);   or the dispute but a few hours ago *which of them is accounted to be greatest* (*St. Luke* xxii, 24);   or Simon Peter's imminent denial.   The divine watchfulness has not only to keep them from evil contacts, but to set them free from the hold which the Evil One has upon them even now.

And we, who are also disciples, know how true this is of ourselves.   Can we even say with confidence that we are not from the world (which " lieth in the evil one ") as He is not from the world?   Yes — if we have at all received and observed His word, we can say that.   But the Evil One (person or principle matters little) has a grip upon us: " deliver us from the Evil One ".

*

16-19. " From the world they are not, as I myself am not from the world.   Consecrate them in the truth;   ' thy word is truth '.   As me thou didst send into the world, I also sent them into the world. And for their sakes I consecrate myself, that they also may be consecrated in truth."

From the world they are not, as I myself am not from the world; the declaration of verse 14 is repeated as an introduction to the thought of consecration which immediately follows; for the consecration of the disciples, which is dependent on that of their Master, is bestowed on the same ground; their qualification to receive it is the same in kind as His, however far it falls short in degree.

Consecrate them. The Greek word is that used for the consecration of a sacrificial victim or the hallowing of a man for sacred work. It refers more to the external benediction and commission than to the inward character. As contrasted with " purify " it is positive, not negative. To " purify " is to cleanse from uncleanness, such as would disqualify a man for consecration; to " consecrate " is to equip a man already qualified with the commission to work for God. The disciples are already cleansed or purified on account of the word which Christ has spoken to them (xv, 3); their life now has its spring in that word, so that they are not *from the world.* Therefore He prays the Father to *consecrate them* for their work of witness.

Because their work is witness, their consecration is *in the truth.* So St. Paul tells his converts at Thessalonica that God chose them " as first-fruits unto salvation in consecration of spirit and faith in the truth " (*II Thessalonians* ii, 13). The truth, which is given to them and to which they are to bear witness, is, so to speak, the medium and atmosphere of their consecration. So the word both cleanses and consecrates, and the identity of the cleansing and consecrating word and the truth is then clinched by the citation of *Psalm* cxix, 142 — *Thy word is truth.*

Now follows the purpose and occasion of this consecration: *As me thou didst send into the world, I also sent them into the world*. The Apostolic mission and ministry which originates in the sending of the Son by the Father is continued in the sending of the Apostles by the Son. Once again the Lord appears as true Mediator. The Father : the Son : : the Son : the Apostles. Down the centuries and across the continents and oceans the Apostolate continues, till " the consummation of the age " (*St. Matthew* xxviii, 20). Soon He will repeat this apostolic commission when He breathes upon them the Holy Spirit (xx, 21, 22). But now He turns to Himself, the channel through whom this ministry of salvation flows forth from the Father.

And for their sakes I consecrate myself, that they also may be consecrated in truth. Wonderful words! *For their sakes* He had come into the world and spoken as *never man spake* (vii, 46): now *for their sakes* — for our sakes — He consecrates Himself. No other could do that. I cannot consecrate myself; Aaron could not consecrate himself. But He, who is " a High Priest for ever ", not by any succession but " after the order of Melchizedek " (*Hebrews* vi, 20; vii, 2, 3), consecrates Himself. But to what end? Is not the Father's mission His consecration? No; something more is now called for. He has fulfilled that mission. He has glorified the Father on the earth by finishing the work which He had given Him to do (4). There remains the glory which is attained in that departure from earth which is called death. To this He now commits Himself. But this death, which to ordinary observers will seem an execution, is in its true reality a sacrifice. The priest consecrates the victim; *I consecrate myself*.

That they also may be consecrated in truth. His mission and His consecration are alike mediatorial. Their end is not in themselves, but in their effect, which is the union of those whom the Father has given

Him (6) alike with His mission and with His consecration. The principle applies to all Christians,
pre-eminently to those who are by office commissioned
as witnesses, but by no means to them alone.

Consecrated in truth: truly consecrated, and commissioned as an agent of truth. That is our vocation;
to most of us it is still our aspiration rather than our
experience; the power to translate that aspiration
into experience flows from the self-consecration of
Christ to that perfect obedience which He con-
summated on the Cross.

*

(3) THE SON, THE DISCIPLES AND THE WORLD (20-26)

20-23. " But not concerning these alone do I ask, but also concerning
those who believe on me through their word, that they all may be
one, as thou, Father, in me and I in thee, that they also may be in
us, that the world may believe that thou didst send me. And the
glory which thou hast given to me I have given to them, that they
may be one as we are one — I in them and thou in me, that they
may be perfected into one, that the world may come to recognise that thou didst send me and didst love them as thou didst
love me."

Not concerning these alone do I ask. His prayer was
for the disciples for their own sake, but also for the
sake of others whom they would win to discipleship. We are to our Lord at once ends in ourselves,
and means to other ends; it is dangerous for us to
forget either. *But also concerning those who believe on
me through their word. Who believe;* present tense;
wherever there is a true disciple, there are others whom
he has won or is winning. The circle of the Church
widens for ever from the moment of the Incarnation
till it reaches the limits of the world. *Through their
word* — for " belief cometh of hearing, and hearing
by the word of Christ " (*Romans* x, 17), the word
which the Father gave to the Son and the Son to His
disciples (8, 14). *That they all may be one* — the

spiritual unity which is perfect mutual love is to include
these newer converts also and bind them into that
fellowship which answers to the perfection of love in
the Godhead — *as thou, Father, in me and I in thee,
that they also may be in us.*

Once again we are reminded how transcendent is
that theme which alone deserves the name of Christian unity. We meet in committees and construct
our schemes of union; in face of the hideous fact of
Christian divisions we are driven to this; but how
paltry are our efforts compared with the call of God!
The way to the union of Christendom does not lie
through committee-rooms, though there is a task of
formulation to be done there. It lies through personal
union with the Lord so deep and real as to be comparable with His union with the Father. For the
prayer is not directly that believers may be " one " in
the Father and the Son, though by a natural error an
early scribe introduced that thought. The prayer is
that they may be in us. If we are in the Father and the
Son, we certainly shall be one, and our unity will
increase our effective influence in the world. But
it is not our unity as such that has converting power;
it is our incorporation into the *true Vine* as branches
in which the divine life is flowing. When all believers
are truly " in Christ ", then their witness will have
its destined effect — *that the world may believe that
thou didst send me.*

For the salvation of the world is the goal. *God so
loved the world* (iii, 16). The divine " election " (*I
chose you out of the world*, xv, 19), whereby some
have spiritual opportunities which are denied to others,
does not operate for the sake of the elect alone; they
have those opportunities in order that, by use of them,
they may win others to the divine love. The purpose
of election, as of judgement, is " that he might have
mercy upon all " (*Romans* xi, 32). The Father sent
the Son, the Son sent the Apostles, the Apostles sent

those who should carry on the message till at last the world should believe — what? That the Father sent the Son. For in this Mission lies the one hope of the world; and the world's supreme need is to discover that its hope lies there.

Now the condition and consequence of this perfect unity are unfolded. *And the glory which thou hast given to me I have given to them.* We know now what that glory is — absolute love in perfect self-expression; this, in face of the selfishness of the world, is the Cross, but when the divine love has by its self-sacrifice won its response, it is the perfect happiness of love given and returned. This, of which the Cross is one aspect and the New Jerusalem is the other aspect, is what the Father eternally bestows upon the Son, and the Son historically bestows upon His disciples.

The purpose and consequence of that gift of *glory* is that the unity of the Godhead may be reproduced in them — in us — *that they may be one as we are one.* The possibility of this, which seems so unattainable, is grounded in the position and work of Christ as the perfect Mediator — *I in them and thou in me* (for the Father: the Son : : the Son : His disciples); and this unity is, after all, the fulfilment of their own destiny: *that they may be perfected into one.* That fellowship of love is the end for which we were created and for which our nature as God fashioned it is designed. By His Incarnation the Lord Jesus not only cancels the consequences of sin and eliminates sin itself, but carries forward the purpose of God in the creation of man to its fulfilment. The word translated *perfected* does not primarily suggest ethical perfection but complete realisation of ideal or type; a fair rendering of the original would be: *that they may become full grown into one.*

Plainly this purpose of God in creation cannot be complete in a selection of individuals. So we return to the great hope *that the world may come to recognise*

that thou didst send me; only now it is *recognise*, not
believe as in 21; for now there is offered something
for the world to see, namely *the glory* which the Father
gave to the Son, and the Son to the disciples (22), the
glory which is absolute love in perfect self-expression.
So through the perfecting into one of the disciples and
their converts (23) the world is enabled progressively
to *recognise* the divine activity at work — *that thou
didst send me*, but also *that thou didst love them as thou
didst love me*. It is the manifestation of God's love
toward us in our mutual love which shall at last convert
the world.

*

24. " Father, as for that which thou hast given to me — I will that
where I am they also may be with me, that they may behold the
glory that is mine, which thou hast given to me because thou lovedst
me before the foundation of the world. "

Father: the simple address without epithet (contrast 11 and 25) suggests the intimately personal
nature of this prayer. He does not now *ask*, but
states a desire or longing for the eternal companionship of His friends in the Father's presence. He has
given to them the glory which He received from the
Father (22), and now yearns for fellowship with them
in the fruition of it. *As for that which thou hast given
to me:* again, as in 2 and vi, 37 and 39, the neuter
singular is substituted for the masculine plural to suggest the unity of the fellowship which was the Father's
gift to the Son. *I will that where I am they also may
be with me.* He came not to do His own will;
but He knows that this for which He longs is
the Father's will; so at the height of His prayer of
self-dedication He can present to the Father His own
desire. Indeed it is only at such a moment, when
we have no desire which is not His, that we can
safely and confidently present in our prayers our own
desires.

That they may behold the glory that is mine. The word *behold* is that which we have often rendered by " notice " or " take note of ". Here the more exalted tone is essential, but the idea is still that of careful attention, which, in this case, must be adoring contemplation. *The glory that is mine;* for it is not what any had ever dared to call " glory " before; yet beside it the lustre of all other glory is tarnished and tawdry. This glory is not His own; it shines through Him (i, 14); it is the Father's gift — *which thou hast given to me because thou lovedst me before the foundation of the world.* The perfect love of the Father for the Son and of the Son for the Father — which is the Holy Spirit — is the glory of the Godhead. It is eternal. In the earthly sojourn of the Son it is historically disclosed; but itself it is eternal — *before the world was* (5), *before the foundation of the world* (24).

The prayer of the Lord for His disciples is that they may *behold*, may contemplate with adoration, that glory. Is there an element of hope for His own delight in their full understanding of Him? There is no reason to exclude that thought, for such delight is a fruit of love. But His longing that they may be with Him and behold the glory which the Father eternally bestows on Him is not chiefly for His sake but for theirs; for this is the Vision of God, the Beatific Vision, the infinite joy of the finite soul.

*

25-26. " Righteous Father, the world did not recognise thee, but I recognised thee and these recognised that thou didst send me. And I made known to them thy Name and will make it known, that the love wherewith thou lovedst me may be in them and I in them. "

Righteous Father: the more personal appeal is made and ended. Now He addresses the Father as *righteous* or " just ", because He must needs return from the ultimate hope of a converted and believing world

(23) to the immediate need of the present.   The
world still rejects the light, and only the Lord and His
disciples have recognised the Father — He by direct
vision, they through the manifestation in the Incarnate
Son (vi, 46 and xiv, 9).   It is justice which requires a
discrimination between the world and the disciples, so
that here again as earlier (9) the Lord's concern is for
these, that the divine love and the Lord Himself may
be in them.   *The world did not recognise thee*;   the
opportunity was given, but the blind world could not
take it.   *But I recognised thee*;   the Lord's unique
apprehension of the Father is the basis of all knowledge of God that comes through the revelation in
the Son.   *And these recognised that thou didst send me*;
they have not been blind to the revelation, though as
yet their understanding of it is limited to a realisation
that their Lord is one sent from God (xvi, 30).   The
Lord has set the truth before them;   but they have
not yet fully grasped it;   so He will continue to set it
before them;   indeed His supreme disclosure of it is
now imminent.   *I made known to them thy Name*;   the
Name is the manifested character.   His whole life
and teaching has been making this known;   but there
remains a still fuller manifestation.   *God so loved the
world* (iii, 16);   the disciples had not yet seen fully
how He loved;   that was only now about to appear;
not yet can the Revealer cry *It is finished* (xix, 30); and
so *I made known to them thy Name and will make it
known* — upon the Cross.

And what is the purpose of that revelation?
Nothing less than this: *that the love wherewith thou
lovedst me* — the very life of Triune Godhead — *may
be in them and I in them*.   We are called to be " par-
takers of the divine nature " (*II Peter* i, 4), of that
love which is the essence of Deity.   This becomes
possible through the indwelling in us of the Son — *I
in them* — not by any spontaneous or laborious ascent
of our own spirits.   How then does the Love of God

effect His entrance into our self-centred and hardened hearts? If we read on we shall see.

*

xviii, 1. When he had said these things Jesus went forth with his disciples over the brook Kedron, where was a garden, into which he entered, himself and his disciples.

That garden was Gethsemane.

ACT IV

THE CONFLICT OF LIGHT WITH DARKNESS

Chapters XVIII and XIX

THE CONFLICT OF LIGHT WITH DARKNESS

HITHERTO the Evangelist has told his story with its spiritual meaning for every reader foremost in his mind. He has recorded acts of the Lord, but always for the sake of a lesson taught by them — a lesson brought out by a discourse contained in the narrative itself, as the discourse on the Bread of Life draws out the meaning of the Feeding of the Five Thousand. The whole section which I have called Act III (Chapters XIII–XVII) consists of discourse, though in Chapter XIII this is connected with the Feet Washing; and in those discourses as thus recorded the living Lord is speaking to our souls, as once He spoke to the disciples and to His Father.

But now, in Act IV (Chapters XVIII and XIX) and in Act V (Chapter XX) we have narrative without any interpreting discourse. It is possible, no doubt, to seek personal application here as elsewhere, to consider how far the sin of Judas or Peter or Caiaphas or Pilate is to be found in our own hearts; and this is profitable in its place. But it seems that St. John would here direct our minds away from ourselves altogether to the Lord; we are now not to meditate, but to contemplate; for the *crisis of this world* (XII) is come, and the conflict between light and darkness is being fought out, until the Victor cries " *It is finished* " (XIX), even until His victory is made manifest (XX). What most benefits us now is not to seek " personal applications " but to become wholly concentrated upon the Word of God as He goes forth " to judge and to make war " (*Revelation* xix, 11).

Consequently we shall follow St. John's own lead and from this point onwards seek only to understand the objective fact itself — the fact which justified the triumphant cry, *It is finished*.

CHAPTER XVIII

(1) The Arrest (1-11)

1. When he had said these things Jesus went forth with his disciples over the brook Kedron, where was a garden, into which he entered, himself and his disciples.

Jesus went forth from the Temple Court where He had consecrated Himself, to the *garden* where in natural reaction from the mood of exaltation He must face the stark reality of what, by His own choice, awaits Him. We know the prayer that He uttered in that garden, and the stress which accompanied it (*St. Mark* xiv, 32-36; *St. Luke* xxii, 39-44). St. John does not record the prayer, but he alludes to it (11). It is enough to say that He went across the brook Kedron, *where was a garden.*

*

2-11. And Judas also who was betraying him knew the place, because many a time Jesus and his disciples assembled there. So Judas, having received the cohort and officers from the chief priests and from the Pharisees, cometh thither with torches and lanterns and weapons. Jesus, therefore, knowing all the things that were coming upon him, went forth and said to them " Whom seek ye? " They answered him " Jesus of Nazareth ". He said to them " I am he ". (And there stood with them also Judas who was betraying him.) When therefore he said to them " I am he " they went backwards and fell to the ground. Again therefore he asked them " Whom seek ye? " And they said " Jesus of Nazareth ". Jesus answered " I told you that I am he; if then it is I whom ye seek, let these go their way " (that the word might be fulfilled which he said, " Those whom thou hast given me, I destroyed of them not one "). Simon Peter, therefore, having a sword drew it and struck the high priest's slave and cut off his right ear; and the name of the slave was Malchus. Jesus therefore said to Peter " Put the sword into the sheath; the cup which my Father has given me, am I not to drink it? "

Judas who was betraying him; the tense in the original emphasises the fact that Judas was at that moment engaged on his work of treason; it is not a mere description of him as the traitor. The Lord had often used this garden as a place of resort and rendezvous. He does not go there because the traitor will look there first; but neither does He avoid it for that reason. He goes His own way, and lets Judas act as he will.

Judas has been to the Sanhedrin and has received from them not only their own " officers ", that is, the Temple police, but also a contingent of troops from Fort Antonia — *the cohort* — for the loan of which the chief priests must have already made arrangements with Pilate. As they approach, the Lord arouses His sleeping disciples (*St. Mark* xiv, 41-43) and goes forth to meet them. They had come prepared to search for Him in the bushes of the garden; otherwise, with the full moon shining, there would be no use for *torches and lanterns*. But there is no need to search. The Lord knows all that is coming upon Him. He has faced it all, and is assured that it is the Father's will; therefore He accepts it, and makes even His arrest a willing offering: *Jesus, knowing all the things that were coming upon him, went forth and said to them " Whom seek ye? "* He comes forth, as one disturbed in meditation, to ask what this turmoil means. At first He is not recognised; instead of saying " We seek you ", *they answered him, " Jesus of Nazareth ".* The name is partly description, partly an expression of contempt; the latter element is emphasised by the actual expression used — *Jesus the Nazarene. He saith to them " I am he "* or *" I am "*; again we have the phrase which may mean no more than " I am the man you describe ", as in ix, 9, but may also be the sacred Name of God. To the soldiers it meant the former; to us it means also the latter. We are the world to whom our God comes forth in the Person of

Jesus the Nazarene saying " Whom seek ye? " The world is groping after its true leader; He offers Himself; and the world, after yielding for a moment to the impact of His divinity, arrests Him and crucifies Him.

The course chosen by the Lord in thus offering Himself to them has put Judas out of action. He had given the sign that would indicate the Prisoner (*St. Mark* xiv, 44); but there is no need of that. For the moment he can do nothing but stand there with the rest, and the Beloved Disciple saw him: *there stood with them also Judas who was betraying him.*

The effect of the Lord's words, and His dignity as He exposes Himself to His enemies, overpower them for the moment. They drop back, and some even fall down as the crowd shrinks away from the helpless yet dominating Figure: *when therefore he said to them " I am he " they went backwards and fell to the ground.* The Lord therefore repeats his question — " *Whom seek ye?* " They are able to repeat their answer — " *Jesus of Nazareth* ". *Jesus answered, " I told you that I am he; if then it is I whom ye seek, let these go their way* ". He alone is able now to bear what is coming; He will not have His disciples involved. Peter's loyal action, about to be recorded, is quite as far from the divine purpose in this scene as are his disloyal words in the court of the High Priest's house. The disciples must be protected, not only from the physical danger but from the insidious spiritual perils that accompanied it. Here was one instance of the care of the Good Shepherd for His flock, justifying the claim " *Those whom thou hast given me, I destroyed of them not one* " (xvii, 12). The Greek means more than *lost*, but hardly so much as *destroyed*; it does, however, represent an action on the part of the Lord, not a deprivation in which He was purely passive. The change of phrase from *not one of them perished* or *was destroyed* to *I destroyed* or *lost not one* is appropriate. If the Lord had at this stage associated the disciples with Himself, He would have been exposing them to trials beyond their strength, and would have become responsible for their failure.

It was, no doubt, at this point that Judas came forward and carried out his promise to the soldiers. His kiss was not only traitorous but futile, for the Lord has not left it to Judas to make known his identity. With Judas come the soldiers and the officers of the Temple police. In the turmoil *Simon Peter having a sword drew it and struck the high priest's slave and cut off his right ear.* He had declared his readiness to give his life for his Master (xiii, 37), and now he shews that this was true; he begins to fight though the odds against him are overwhelming. He draws his sword — there were only two swords among them all (*St. Luke* xxii, 38), but we are not surprised that Simon Peter had one of them — and slashes at one of the new-comers. It is not a soldier at all, but only a slave of the High Priest. The slave swings aside, and the blow aimed at the crown of his head cuts off his ear. *The name of the slave was Malchus*; a realistic touch due to the memory of an eye-witness who knew the High Priest's household (see 15); but perhaps this Malchus was known in the early Church as a convert, so that his name was a matter of general interest; that the action of the Lord in healing his wound at such a moment (*St. Luke* xxii, 51) should begin the process of his conversion is easily intelligible; but of all this we have no evidence.

The words of the Lord are sublime: *Put the sword into the sheath; the cup which my Father has given me, am I not to drink it?* We recall the prayer that this Cup might pass from Him; we recall the Agony and Bloody Sweat; but He knows that the Father Himself is offering the Cup; none shall hinder His drinking it.

*

(2) The Ecclesiastical Trials (12-27)

12-14. The cohort, therefore, and the captain and the officers of the Jews seized Jesus and bound him, and led him to Annas first; for he was father-in-law to Caiaphas, who was high priest that year; and Caiaphas was he who counselled the Jews that it was expedient that one man should die on behalf of the people.

The Roman troops and their commanding officer, with the Temple police, make the arrest and bind their Prisoner according to their custom; no more need be intended than a binding of the hands behind the back — the equivalent to our handcuffs. Then *they led him to Annas first*. Only St. John tells this; it is one of the facts recorded by him alone which make intelligible the Synoptic narrative where it otherwise would be, at best, obscure (see Introduction, pp. xi and xii). St. Mark records a trial before the High Priest during the night (*St. Mark* xiv, 53-65) followed by a " consultation " of the " chief priests with the elders and scribes and the whole council " in the morning (xv, 1). This is possible, but not easily intelligible. St. John tells us that the earlier trial was an informal enquiry at the house of Annas, at which the decision was reached, though sentence could not there be pronounced. Then, very early in the morning, the Sanhedrin met in full session and rapidly confirmed in legal verdict and sentence what had been informally decided during the night. (St. Luke, who does not record the informal enquiry, is probably right in saying the crucial question (xxii, 67 and 70) was put in the later and formal trial; but this would be a repetition of what had happened earlier: cf. *St. Mark* xiv, 61 and 62; and *St. Matthew* xxvi, 63 and 64. St. Mark and St. Luke give no name to the High Priest in whose house the earlier enquiry took place (xiv, 53); St. Matthew by a natural mistake inserts the name of Caiaphas (xxvi, 57). In fact this enquiry took place at the house of Annas, as St. John is careful to make plain.)

*He was father-in-law to Caiaphas, who was high
priest that year*; so St. John accounts for the fact that
he presided over this informal enquiry. He had been
High Priest himself, and was head of the high-priestly
family. Moreover, he controlled from the background
his various sons and sons-in-law who successively held
the office. But there may be more involved than this.
Annas was deposed from the office of High Priest by
Valerius Gratus, the predecessor of Pilate as Pro-
curator of Judaea. It is possible that he himself and
a section of Jewish opinion regarded this act as an
unwarrantable intrusion of the secular State in the
affairs of the Church, and consequently held that he
was still *de jure* High Priest. The acts of Rome must
needs be accepted for all legal transactions; but it may
be that the assent of Annas was thought necessary to
give spiritual validity to the acts of the Sanhedrin,
even though Caiaphas presided at its formal session.
This would account for the very curious expressions
in *St. Luke* iii, 2 (" under the high-priesthood of Annas
and Caiaphas "), and *Acts* iv, 6 (" Annas the high priest
was there, and Caiaphas and John and Alexander and
as many as were of the kindred of the high priest ").

The mention of Caiaphas revives the memory of
that cynic's counsel which was unwittingly a statement of divine truth (xi, 50): *it is expedient that one man
should die on behalf of the people.* Both his cynicism and
the divine truth are now to be displayed openly.

*

St. Peter's First Denial

15-18. And there followed Jesus Simon Peter and another disciple.
That disciple was known to the high priest and went in with Jesus
into the courtyard of the high priest, but Peter was standing at the
door outside. So the other disciple, the acquaintance of the high
priest, went out and spoke to the door-keeper and brought in Peter.
The maid who kept the door saith therefore to Peter " Thou art
not, surely, also one of this man's disciples? " He said " I am not ".

And there were standing there the slaves and the officers, having made a fire of charcoal, because it was cold; and they were warming themselves; and there was also Peter among them, standing and warming himself.

The story is very vivid, though one point in it is notoriously difficult. After the arrest, when all the disciples " left him and fled " (*St. Mark* xiv, 50), St. Peter "followed afar off " (*St. Mark* xiv, 54). So much St. Mark knew from St. Peter's narration of his own recollection; also that somehow St. Peter found access to the courtyard of the High Priest. St. John tells us that another disciple followed with Peter; no doubt this is the Beloved Disciple, John the son of Zebedee. But he goes on — *that disciple was known to the high priest.* This phrase has been much discussed, and is the point of notorious difficulty referred to above. But John the son of Zebedee was, on his mother's side, of priestly descent; his mother was Salome, the sister of the Virgin Mary; they were related to Elizabeth, who is described as " of the daughters of Aaron " (*St. Luke* i, 5). It is possible at least that John came at times to perform priestly duties at Jerusalem, and that this is the origin of the statement of Polycrates that he was a priest and wore the Petalon — a gold plate attached to the front of the priestly turban or mitre (*Exodus* xxviii, 36); the same is said of St. James the Just (a " brother " of the Lord) and of St. Mark; the latter is shewn to be of Levite connexion by the comparison of *Acts* iv, 36 and *Colossians* iv, 10). But even if St. John was not himself a priest, he may have been often in Jerusalem, and had opportunity to become known to the High Priest; there was much commerce between the fishermen of Galilee and the capital; some have suggested that this family, which was sufficiently prosperous to employ hired servants, had an establishment in Jerusalem to which St. John was commonly attached.

All of this is speculation, but supplies reason for

accepting without hesitation the simple statement of
fact that *that disciple was known to the high priest,* so
that the door-keeper readily admitted him among
those who *followed Jesus* into *the courtyard of the high
priest.* It is likely that this was a courtyard into which
different houses opened, one being that of Annas,
another that of Caiaphas. When St. John had made
his way in among the crowd, and was able to take note
of what had happened, he found that the admission
allowed to himself had been refused to the markedly
Galilean Peter (*St. Mark* xiv, 70), so that *Peter was*
(still) *standing at the door outside.* So St. John used the
opportunity due to the fact that he was an acquaintance of the High Priest to speak to the door-keeper
and get leave to bring in Peter. The maid knew, presumably, that St. John was a disciple and says in
effect " Surely you are not another of them? " The
form of question is that which " expects the answer
No "; but it is satirically spoken; the combination of
the form and the tone constitutes a temptation which
finds Peter unprepared; and he slides into the place
prepared for him: " Not another, surely "; " Oh,
no ". So sudden and so easy! But now it will be very
hard to go back and give the loyal answer when the
direct challenge comes (25-27).

We do not always see how unwitting was Peter's
first denial. Of course a perfect loyalty would have
avoided it. But we all know with what fatal ease we
accept a position prepared for us if it is presented
suddenly and offers a refuge from many troubles. And
then the harm is done! The act seemed so nearly
innocent; the avoidance of its guilty consequence is
so very hard.

Anyhow, Peter is there now among *the slaves and
the officers,* that is, the Temple police; it is cold and
they have made a fire; and Peter was there with them,
standing and warming himself.

*

19-24. The high priest, therefore, asked Jesus about his disciples and his teaching. Jesus answered him " I have spoken openly to the world; I always taught in synagogue and in the temple, where all the Jews come together, and in secret I spake nothing. Why dost thou ask me? Ask them who have heard what I spake to them; behold, they know the things which I said." And when he had said these things, one who was standing by, one of the officers, struck Jesus with his open hand, saying " Is that the way for thee to answer the high priest? " Jesus answered him, " If I spake ill, bear witness of the ill; but if well, why dost thou smite me? " So Annas sent him bound to Caiaphas the high priest.

The purpose of this informal enquiry is to find evidence which can be presented at the formal session of the Sanhedrin a few hours later, so that a verdict and sentence can then be pronounced at once, and the case sent on to Pilate. The only charge that is likely to move Pilate to action is that of sedition; and it was a political argument to which he ultimately yielded (xix, 12). So the first point of enquiry concerns the disciples, and what was the teaching given to them: *the high priest asked Jesus about his disciples and his teaching*. Of course he hoped by cross-examination to elicit something which would shew that the Lord was training a group of rebels. The Triumphal Entry had looked like a serious rising and had created consternation among the Pharisees (xi, 19). But the Lord's answer gives him no ground for encouragement. Instead of answering the question, he challenges the method of the enquiry. The proper course was to formulate a charge and call witnesses, when (incidentally) the Jewish custom would require witnesses for the defence to be called first. What Annas is attempting is to inveigle the Prisoner into giving evidence against Himself. This He will not do. In His answer the first pronoun is very emphatic: " *I* am not a secret conspirator "; *I have spoken openly to the world. I always taught in synagogue and in the temple* (as we might say, in Church or in the Cathedral), *where all the Jews come together, and in secret I spake nothing.* The teaching given in the Upper Room and in the Temple Court, contained in Chapters XIII to XVII, was in substance no more than an articulation of what He had often said in public. So there are no secrets to be disclosed. If Annas wishes for evidence about His teaching, he can obtain it in the usual way. *Ask them who have heard what* (it was that) *I spake to them; behold, they know the things which I said.*

That this enquiry was irregular and informal is proved by the next episode; it is incredible that one of the police should smack the prisoner's face (for that is what the words mean) during a formal trial before the Sanhedrin. *When he had said these things, one who was standing by, one of the officers, struck Jesus with his open hand, saying " Is that the way for thee to answer the high priest? "* The Lord remains perfectly calm, recalling the policeman, as He had recalled the High Priest, to the method appropriate to a legal enquiry: *If I spake ill, bear witness of the ill; but if well, why dost thou smite me?*

St. John does not recall the rest of the trial — either the attempt to find witnesses who can prove that Jesus was preparing a riot aiming at the destruction of the Temple, which He would then replace with a miraculous structure of His own (*St. Mark* xiv, 58), though he has told us of the saying of Jesus which was twisted into this (ii, 19); or the direct question of the High Priest, though to this too he alludes, in so far as the Jews demand of Pilate the death-penalty because of the Lord's claim to be the Son of God (xix, 7). Though this latter is not what would be most welcome for submission to Pilate, it can be made to serve, for it can be twisted into a political charge (compare xix, 7, with xix, 12). *So Annas sent him bound to Caiaphas the high priest.*

*

St. Peter's Later Denials

25-27. And there was Simon Peter standing and warming himself. They said to him therefore " Surely thou art not also one of his disciples? " That man denied it and said " I am not ". There saith one of the slaves of the high priest, being a kinsman of him whose ear Peter cut off, " Did not I see thee in the garden with him? " Again therefore Peter denied, and immediately a cock crew.

We are taken back to the courtyard where Peter is standing with the rest. One of these asks him the same question as the maid had put to him — again with the suggestion that he is not one of the disciples; and again he yields to the suggestion. But then one notices him who recalls his features; he had seen that face in the garden; but Peter again denies. *And immediately the cock crew.*

St. John has a double purpose in this narrative — first, to point out the contrast between the serene calm of the Lord, whose constancy was leading Him to torture and death, and the frightened inconstancy of the disciple, who had nothing worse to fear than mockery; secondly, to offer some excuse for Simon Peter by shewing how easy it was for him to slip. With the first object in view he breaks the story of the denials into two parts, and takes us backwards and forwards between the room where the Lord stands with bound hands before Annas and the courtyard where Peter stretches out his free hands to the charcoal fire in the brazier. With the second object, he gives the actual tone of the first two questions to Peter, and passes rapidly over his actual fall; there is no word here of cursing and swearing, as there was in Peter's own story of his shame (*St. Mark* xiv, 71). St. John does not want to exhibit St. Peter's shame, but to warn us by his example how very easily we slide towards denial of our Lord.

Everyone who has found himself " in a tight place " and seized an unexpected opportunity of escape will recognise the difference in the force of temptation

latent in the two forms of question, " You aren't one
of them, are you? " and " You are one of them, aren't
you? "   To deny the second is to refuse a direct
challenge; it was what Peter did the third time. To
accept the suggestion of the first is scarcely more than
a refusal to look for trouble. The suggestion is that he
is not likely to be a disciple, and no one will suppose
he is unless he says so; he had little more to do than
to let well alone. But that little more is fatal If the
third question had come first, perhaps he could have
met it with truth and loyalty. Peter was not one to be
browbeaten into apostasy! But he was one to fear
laughter, and to take a way of avoiding it when it was
offered him.

Meanwhile the Lord was being sent from Annas to
Caiaphas, that is, to the Sanhedrin where Caiaphas
is president. He must pass through the courtyard,
and on the way " the Lord turned and looked on
Peter ".   At the same moment a cock crew (27;
St. Luke xxii, 60).

Probably the cock's crow was not the cry of a
bird but the trumpet sounding the " cock-crow "
which marked the transition from the third watch of
the night, called " Cock-crowing ", to the fourth, called
" Early "; the four night watches were Late, Midnight, Cock-crowing and Early. This makes the
Lord's prediction in xiii, 38, more natural; before
" cock-crowing " was a definite indication of time.

Time had been carefully calculated; it was important to secure Pilate's sentence early, so that the
actual crucifixion should be carried through and finished
before the day of the feast should begin at 6 P.M. (cf.
xix, 31). The proceedings in the Sanhedrin would
be very short — just the one question, " Art thou the
Christ? " which the Prisoner cannot refuse to answer,
and by answering which He must involve himself in
the guilt of blasphemy. So at the moment of " cock-
crow ", as the sound of the trumpet rings out, the

L

enquiry before Annas is closed; the Sanhedrin meets
— it is the earliest hour at which a condemnation to
death would be technically legal; and at once the
Prisoner is led to Pilate, in that phase of the night
which the trumpet ushers in and which is called
Early.

*

(3) THE TRIAL BEFORE PILATE (xviii, 28–xix, 16)

The trial before Pilate is divided into sections by
the movements of Pilate in and out of the Praetorium.
Westcott describes them as follows :

1. Without the Praetorium. The Jews claim the execution
   of their sentence (xviii, 28-32).
2. Within the Praetorium. "The good confession."
   Christ a King (33-37).
3. Without the Praetorium. First declaration of innocence.
   Barabbas (38-40).
4. Within the Praetorium. Scourging; mockery (xix, 1-3).
5. Without the Praetorium. Second and third declarations
   of innocence. "Ecce Homo "; "Son of God " (4-7).
6. Within the Praetorium. The source of authority and
   from this the measure of guilt (8-11).
7. Without the Praetorium. Conviction overpowered: the
   King abjured: the last sentence (12-16).

*

1. Without the Praetorium. The Jews claim the
execution of their sentence (xviii, 28-32):

They lead Jesus therefore from Caiaphas into the palace; and it was
Early; and themselves they did not enter into the palace, that they
might not be defiled but might eat the Passover. Pilate therefore
went out to them outside, and saith " What accusation do ye bring
against this man? " They answered and said to him " If this man
were not doing evil, we should not have delivered him to thee ".
Pilate therefore saith to them " Take him yourselves, and according
to your law judge him ". The Jews said to him " To us it is not
allowed to put anyone to death " — that the word of Jesus might be
fulfilled which he said signifying by what manner of death he was
about to die.

They lead Jesus therefore from Caiaphas to the palace, that is, from the Court of the Sanhedrin to the Praetorium, the house of the Governor. *And it was Early;* it was, in fact, a little after 3 A.M., at which hour the trumpet had sounded Cock-crow. *And themselves they did not enter into the palace, that they might not be defiled but might eat the Passover.* They were demanding the crucifixion of the Lord of Glory, but of course no one thought of that as defilement; to enter the heathen ruler's house would be defilement! (A besetting sin of all of us, who are concerned with the ordering of religious life and worship, is the loss of proportion and perspective, and the attribution of primary importance to secondary or even to tertiary and quaternary concerns!) But as they would not go in, Pilate must needs come out, and his frequent movements backwards and forwards are due to their scrupulosity. It is natural to suppose that this added to Pilate's contemptuous irritation, and made him the more determined to impose upon these tiresome priests a good deal of humiliation before he granted their request. *Pilate therefore went out to them outside, and saith " What accusation do ye bring against this man? "*

Pilate must have known that the chief priests were going to bring before him a man whose execution would be demanded. He had lent troops to assist in the arrest; and he is ready at this early hour to hear the case. But he is now to act as judge; he must hear the charge and the defence. Probably he expected a charge of sedition already heard and decided by the Sanhedrin; in that case his own enquiry need not take long; but a definite accusation must be made. There is no reason to suppose that Pilate begins with any other expectation than a speedy verdict of guilty and sentence of death — though it is possible that already he was uneasy as a result of his wife's message (*St. Matthew* xxvii, 19).

Unfortunately for them, the chief priests have no

such charge to bring forward as will at all certainly
lead Pilate to pronounce the death-sentence on which
they are determined. So they try to avoid stating a
definite charge at all. They have held a trial themselves
and have found the Prisoner guilty of evil-doing; that
is enough; Pilate has only to ratify their findings: *If
this man were not doing evil we should not have delivered
him to thee.*

(Doing evil!

> Why, what hath my Lord done?
> What makes this rage and spite?
> He made the lame to run,
> He gave the blind their sight.
> Sweet injuries!
> Yet they at these
> Themselves displease
> And 'gainst him rise.[1])

Pilate was cynical and cruel, but he was not stupid,
and no Roman governor could be without some sense
of the majesty of Roman law. That law entrusted
the death penalty to no local or " native " court, but
reserved it to the representative of Rome. It was not
unknown for a High Priest to be deposed for inflicting
it. If so, it could not be consonant with the law that
the Governor should inflict that penalty at the demand
of the local court without any further trial held by
himself. The reply of the chief priests was, in fact, a
piece of impertinence with which Pilate was very com-
petent to deal. He says in effect " Very well; if you
want the matter settled by the verdict of your court,
let that court pronounce sentence ", knowing, of course,
that their court could not pronounce sentence of death :
Take him yourselves and according to your law judge him.
Now the Jews have to shew their hand, for death alone
will satisfy them: *To us it is not allowed to put any man
to death.* This was itself a grievance, a constant reminder that they were a vassal state. But the result,

[1] Samuel Crossman: see *Songs of Praise*, 127.

as St. John points out, was that the Lord's death when it came fulfilled His own prediction — He was *lifted up from the earth* (xii, 32). If the Sanhedrin condemned any man to death the sentence was carried out by stoning, as in the case of St. Stephen (which was probably after Pilate's disgrace, and Vitellius, who succeeded him, went very far in concessions to the Jewish authorities). None but the Roman authority could crucify.

*

2. Within the Praetorium. "The good confession." Christ a King (33–37) :

Pilate therefore went into the palace again and called Jesus and said to him " Thou — art thou the King of the Jews? " Jesus answered " Of thyself dost thou say this or did others say it to thee concerning me? " Pilate answered " Am I a Jew ? The nation which is thine and the chief priests delivered thee to me. What didst thou do? " Jesus answered " The kingdom which is mine is not from this world; if from this world were the kingdom which is mine, the officers who are mine would be fighting that I should not be delivered to the Jews; but as it is the kingdom which is mine is not from hence ". Pilate therefore saith to him " Then art thou — thou — a king? " Jesus answered " Thou sayest that I am a king. I to this end have been born and to this end am come into the world, that I may bear witness to the truth. Everyone who is from the truth heareth my voice." Pilate saith to him " What is truth? "

Pilate goes back into the palace; no doubt the soldiers have by now taken charge of the Prisoner, and they bring Him too. Pilate is puzzled. He knew that the charge was to be one of sedition; but it has not been made; and the Prisoner does not look like the leader of a serious revolution. Pilate does not constitute his court, but questions the Prisoner himself. The Jews had looked dangerous and if he insisted on sending the case back for such action as the Sanhedrin could take, the consequences might be grave. He had better keep the matter in his own hands now that it has reached them. So he goes behind the general

charge of " doing evil ", which was all that was form-
ally presented, to that which he had been led to
expect. Only now it seems preposterous: *Thou — art
thou the King of the Jews?* The Prisoner does not look
the sort of person to usurp a throne. *Thou* — the
pronoun is so placed as to be most emphatic. It is
evident that Pilate is already convinced that he is not
dealing with a rebel whom Rome need fear. At first
the Lord does not answer the question, but asks
another. He has heard what the chief priests and Jews
had said outside, and it contained no reference to any
claim to Kingship. Has Pilate any information of his
own to suggest that this claim had been made, or was
the statement brought to him from other (that is,
Jewish) quarters? If the former, the information can
be tested; if the latter, the charge should be presented
in proper form, and this the Jews have not done, for
the very good reason that they had not been able to
establish it. *Of thyself dost thou say this? or did others
say it to thee concerning me?* No doubt the High Priest
or his representative had said it when arrangements
were made for the loan of the troops. But that was
a private conversation, of which the course could not
be conveniently made public. Pilate has recourse to
contemptuous indignation: how should he hear of
such things? He is not a Jew or interested in Jewish
concerns, except so far as he had to keep that turbulent
tribe in order. *Am I a Jew?* Again the pronoun is
emphatic. He was a Roman, not one of this despised
race. *The nation which is thine and the chief priests
delivered thee to me. What didst thou do?* It was the
Lord's own people who had brought Him, not a
private group of citizens but the nation as represented
by its own leaders. If He were a champion of national
independence they would be supporting Him; but
somehow He has provoked them to fury: *What
didst thou do?* If He is to be found guilty there must
be an offence of which He is guilty.

The Lord's reply takes up what is the real charge —
that He claims to be the Son of God, the Messiah
(xix, 7; cf. *St. Mark* xiv, 61, 62). In that sense He
does claim to be the *King of Israel* (i, 49); but He has
transformed the conception of that Messianic Kingship. He has royalty, but not what the world means
by royalty, for it neither proceeds from the world nor
is recognisable by the world: *The kingdom which is
mine is not from this world.* He does not claim a
kingdom, but, so to speak, acquiesces in that description of His realm; it is a special kind of kingdom —
the kingdom which is mine — and it is *not from this
world.* He had claimed to be the Messiah; and the
Messiah was a King — but not the sort of King
whose dominion constituted a challenge to the political
authority of Rome. *Not from this world*; the phrase
represents both origin and character due to origin.
An earthly king depends for any effective authority
upon the loyal support of his people and the force
that they can offer in his support. The Messiah
derives His authority from God alone. The quality of
an earthly kingdom is, partly at least, the maintenance
of order by the forcible coercion of malcontents; in
the political sphere this is right, and the earthly State
is rightly entrusted with force wherewith to uphold the
law and prevent the lawless use of force. But the
divine kingdom cannot be content with this; it must
control not only outward conduct but hearts and
wills; its authority is from God, who is Love; its
actuality is in the willing obedience of those whose love
has been called out in response to the manifested love
of God. Consequently it can never fight for its
" vital interests ", because by fighting it betrays them.
The State may rightly fight in national self-defence or
for the maintenance of the law of nations; the Church
may not fight, nor use for its defence or extension any
other method than the lifting up of its King that He
may draw all men unto Him: *If from this world were*

the Kingdom which is mine, the officers who are mine would be fighting that I should not be delivered to the Jews; but as it is the kingdom which is mine is not from hence.

Who are His *officers*? (The word is that used else-where in this narrative for the Temple police. Where-ever it occurs it represents the agents of a king or other public authority.) Can He mean the eleven disciples? One of them had begun to fight with precisely the object here mentioned. But they are evidently helpless against the Temple police and the Roman legionaries. Had He then other *officers* on whom He might call? Yes; "more than twelve legions" of them (*St. Matthew* xxvi, 53). But to call in the heavenly hosts, the "officers" of the "Kingdom of Heaven", to act coercively would be to turn that Kingdom into a Kingdom "from this world". For it is not the differ-ence of the supernatural from the natural that dis-tinguishes Christ's Kingdom; it is the difference between control of conduct by force and control of heart and mind and will by love and truth. His *Kingdom is not from hence.*

Pilate is baffled. It seems the Prisoner does claim kingship after all. *Then art thou — thou — a king?* Once more there is great emphasis on the pronoun. Before the Roman Governor stands a man with hands bound behind His back; He was arrested without difficulty — no more than a scuffle in which one slave was cut on the side of the head; He has no air of pomp or domination; He is, indeed, fearless, and answers the Governor without a trace of subservience; but there is nothing regal about Him: *Then art thou — thou — a king?*

Thou sayest that I am a king; the use of the term "king" was introduced by Pilate. It is his word, not the Prisoner's. It could not be accurately accepted or rejected; to say No would convey one false impression, to say Yes would convey another. So the Lord says in

effect " That is your expression, not mine; but here is
an exact statement of the facts: *I to this end have been
born and to this end am come into the world, that I may
bear witness to the truth. Everyone that is from the truth
heareth my voice.*"

(The expression " Thou sayest " or " Thou hast
said " is not a direct affirmative. To interpret it so in
St. Matthew xxvi, 64 is to lose part of the meaning of
that scene. It is neither Yes nor No, but indicates that
while the phrase used may be quite misleading, yet
there is a sense in which it must be accepted. The
Lord refuses to say that He is or that He is not
the Messiah; for that required a definition of the
Messianic office. But He goes on to say that Daniel's
prophecy is now fulfilled.)

The kingdoms which are *from this world* rest in part
upon falsehood — most conspicuously upon the necessary but false, false but necessary, supposition that the
State really acts in the interest of the whole community, whereas in fact it always acts primarily in the
interest of that section of the community which is
able in practice to work its machinery. It is a pre-
tended community; this is far better than no community at all, which is the only actual alternative
until the Kingdom of God is come. But that Kingdom rests on truth — on the real constitution of the
universe wherein God the *righteous Father* is supreme.
To that *truth*, the real constitution of the universe,
Christ came to *bear witness*; not to beautiful dreams
but to bed-rock reality (cf. *St. Matthew* vii, 24, 25).
*Everyone who is from the truth heareth my voice. From
the truth*; the phrase answers *from this world*; again the
suggestion is of origin and character due to origin.
It is those who are *born from above* who may hope to
see the kingdom of God (iii, 3). Those whose outlook
is directed by the truth, whose judgement springs from
the truth, hear the voice of Christ, *the truth* (xiv, 6).
So He had said that *the sheep that are mine hear my*

voice (x, 27); but of others — *Why do ye not recognise my manner of speech? — because ye cannot hear the word that is mine* (viii, 43). *Everyone who is from the truth heareth my voice.*

This makes Pilate impatient, but also convinces him that the Prisoner is harmless. Abstractions like Truth have nothing to do with a trial for sedition; it is absurd to introduce such a topic; "'*What is truth?*' said jesting Pilate and would not stay for an answer." [1]

But it is better to stay and wait for the answer. We know that answer quite well: *I am the truth* (xiv, 6). Can we say that we are *of* or *from the truth*?

*

3. Without the Praetorium. First declaration of innocence. Barabbas (38-40):

And having said this again he went forth to the Jews and saith to them " I find no crime in him. But there is a custom with you that I should release one prisoner to you at the Passover. Do ye wish then that I release to you the King of the Jews? So they shouted aloud again saying, " Not this man but Barabbas "; and Barabbas was a robber.

Pilate is sure the Prisoner is no criminal. He hopes to deal with the matter by using the custom of releasing one prisoner at the Passover — a strictly limited amnesty. It is a cynical proposal, because if Jesus is innocent He should be acquitted and some other released; the crowd is entitled to claim both Jesus and Barabbas. Perhaps they are irritated at this attempt to get out of granting the amnesty to a real rebel by releasing one who, Pilate says, is no rebel at all. They are bound to be irritated by the scorn implied in the use of the title which the Lord was accused of claiming — *the King of the Jews*. Pilate's device is self-defeating; certainly it fails. The crowd will have its real rebel released: *Not this man but Barabbas.*

[1] Bacon, *Essay on Truth.*

Barabbas was guilty of sedition and of murder (*St. Luke* xxiii, 19); he was an undoubted criminal. But he had defied Rome, and it would be easy for the chief priests to persuade the crowd to demand the release of a bandit-patriot rather than that of One who has only disappointed their nationalist aspirations. Pilate is foiled.

But the choice of Barabbas is more than an episode. It is a symbol. The world has its choice between the real King and the bandit chief; it chooses Barabbas — *and Barabbas was a robber.*

CHAPTER XIX

THE CIVIL TRIAL CONTINUES

4. WITHIN the Praetorium. Scourging; mockery (1-3):

> Then Pilate took Jesus and scourged him. And the soldiers, having plaited a crown out of thorns put it on his head, and cast a purple cloak about him, and were making approach to him and saying " Hail, King of the Jews ! " and they smote him with their open hands.

Pilate goes back into his palace and orders Jesus to be scourged, in the hope that this fearful punishment will satisfy the Jews; for a Roman scourging was a thing of terror. The soldiers who administer the torture enter with zest into a situation which enables them to show their scorn of the Jews. They take the supposed accusation in mock seriousness; they plait a crown or wreath of thorn-twigs to represent the laurel-wreath of a victor; they cast about the lacerated body a coarse scarlet cloak in place of the regal purple; they advance towards Him, one as though to offer homage, another as though to present a petition, saying " *Hail, King of the Jews!* " — fit king (they suggest) for such a people. Then rising from the bended knee they slap Him on the face.

St. John records enough to emphasise the humiliation and the pain; but he does not dwell on it. No record is so little directed towards the harrowing of feelings. All attention is directed towards the bearing of the Sufferer.

*

5. Without the Praetorium. Second and third declarations of innocence. " Ecce Homo "; " Son of God " (4-7):

And Pilate came forth again outside and saith to them " Behold, I
bring him to you outside that ye may recognise that I find no crime
in him ". Jesus therefore came forth outside, wearing the crown of
thorns and the purple cloak. And he saith to them " Behold, the
man ". When therefore the chief priests and the officers saw him
they shouted aloud, saying " Crucify, crucify ". Pilate saith to them
" Take him yourselves and crucify him ; for I do not find crime in
him ". The Jews answered him " We have a law, and according to
the law he ought to die, because he made himself Son of God ".

Pilate now comes out to make his appeal for
sympathy. He hopes that his declaration of the
Prisoner's innocence, coupled with the sight of His
tortured form, may satisfy the rage of the accusers.
(But if He was innocent, why was He scourged?
Even in the method by which Pilate seeks to release
Him there is an outrage upon justice.) So *Jesus came
forth outside, wearing the crown of thorns and the purple
cloak*; He is exhibited in the trappings put on Him
for mockery; and Pilate says *Behold, the Man*.

It is one of those pregnant phrases which cannot be
translated adequately. On Pilate's lips — and so the
Jews would understand it — the words meant " Look
at the poor fellow ". But as we hear them across the
centuries they come charged with another meaning.
Here, in this life of perfect obedience and love; here,
in this courage that bears the worst that hate can do
and is still unfalteringly calm; here, in this love that
is unquenched and undiminished by the desertion of
friends, by the blows and jeers of enemies — here
we see Man fulfilling his true destiny and manifested
as superior to circumstance. " We see not yet all
things subject to man. But we behold him who hath
been made a little lower than the angels, garlanded
for the suffering of death with glory and honour "
(*Hebrews* ii, 8, 9). As the victim was garlanded for
the sacrifice, so Jesus for the Cross — with thorns of
glory and honour.

But the sight of their enemy, as they account Him,
rouses the chief priests and their satellites to frenzy.

They *shout aloud* . . . " *Crucify, crucify* ". Pilate answers with a sneer: "Do it yourselves"; for he knows that they cannot. They hold Him guilty, but will not inflict the only penalty in their power; they demand the death-penalty, which can only be inflicted by the judge who has pronounced Him innocent! "*Take him yourselves and crucify him; for I do not find crime in him.*"

This drives the Jews to state what it is that they have really established against Him. In itself it is blasphemy, and for this He was sentenced to death by the Sanhedrin (*St. Mark* xiv, 61-64); and Pilate may not be prepared to execute for blasphemy; still, the claim of the Lord can be presented as constructive treason (12),[1] and in any case the Jewish law required death as the penalty for such blasphemy as was certainly involved in the claim of Jesus — if it were not the truth! *We have a law, and according to the law he ought to die, because he made himself Son of God.* Yes; when adjured by the High Priest in the name of the living God, He had made the claim that He was " the Christ, the Son of the Blessed " (*St. Mark* xiv, 61). And with the title Son of God goes the title King of Israel (i, 49). The Jews have at any rate stated their full case now.

*

6. Within the Praetorium. The source of authority and from this the measure of guilt (8-11):

When Pilate therefore heard this word he was more afraid, and went into the palace again and saith to Jesus " Whence art thou? " But Jesus did not give him an answer. Pilate therefore saith to him " To me dost thou not speak? Knowest thou not that I have authority to release thee and I have authority to crucify thee? " Jesus answered him " Thou hadst not any authority against me unless it had been given thee from above: for this reason he that delivered me to thee hath greater sin ".

[1] St. Luke represents it as so interpreted from the first: xxiii, 2.

Pilate has little or no respect for the Jewish law, which he regarded, no doubt, as the barbarous code of a contemptible tribe. But, like most heathen cynics, he has a superstitious dread of the supernatural. This Prisoner with His unruffled calm and His talk about a Kingdom of Truth is, no doubt, a fanatic; but there might be something abnormal and supernatural about Him. The title *Son of God* would not for Pilate bear the august meaning which it had for the chief priests, and which made the claim to it blasphemous if it was not true. But this Prisoner might be a son of a god — and the phrase used by the chief priests, where no definite articles are employed, can mean this; Pilate would not want to incur the hostility of a local deity. So he was *more afraid* than he had been till now; he goes inside the palace again, and asks the Prisoner *Whence art thou?*

To that Jesus gives no answer. How could He give one? What is the use of saying to Pilate *I came forth from the Father and am come into the world?* (xvi, 28). With his mind full of stories about gods who married women, and of the offspring of such unions, how can he begin to understand the relation of Jesus, Son of God, to the Father?

Pilate is vexed by His silence; it is in effect contempt of court. *To me dost thou not speak?* It is foolish to despise a judge who has power of life and death: *Knowest thou not that I have authority to release thee and I have authority to crucify thee?* Pilate rightly uses the word which means delegated authority; he thinks of its source as Caesar. But Caesar's authority too is delegated. *Thou hadst not any authority against me unless it had been given thee from above.* Pilate's authority comes, like all real authority, from God. The State has the authority of God in its own sphere; but this is a check as well as a sanction; for the State is confined within its own sphere by the very source of its authority; and even inside that sphere its authority is to execute justice, not to serve the interest of the rulers. If it steps outside its sphere, or uses its power to commit injustice, it becomes at once a usurper. Pilate has authority from God over the Jews and over Jesus as a Jew; he holds it in order to do justice with it; if he uses it for injustice the authority will evaporate. *Therefore he that delivered me to thee hath greater sin.* The sin of Caiaphas is greater because Pilate's authority is from God; and it was the duty of Caiaphas to know and teach as well as do the will of God. But he, the official representative of Israel, the People of God, has had recourse to this heathen, who holds certain authority from God, in order that power conferred by God for the execution of justice may be employed for the perpetration of injustice. That the High Priest, of all men, should say " Though you have found the Prisoner innocent, yet condemn Him to death to gratify our concern for our law ", is far worse than it is for that heathen to execute one apparently deluded fanatic in order to avoid an insurrection.

*

7. Without the Praetorium. Conviction over-powered; the King abjured; the last sentence (12-16):

From that time Pilate was seeking to release him; but the Jews shouted aloud saying " If thou release this man, thou art not a friend of Caesar; everyone who maketh himself a King speaks against Caesar ". Pilate therefore, having heard these words, led Jesus forth outside and sat upon a judgment seat in the place called Pavement but in Hebrew Gabbatha. And it was Preparation Day of the Passover, and it was about the sixth hour. And he saith to the Jews " Behold, your king ". They shouted therefore " Away with him, away with him, crucify him ". Pilate saith to them " Your king — shall I crucify him? " The chief priests answered " We have not a king except Caesar ". So then he delivered him to them to be crucified.

Pilate is now more than ever convinced that the Prisoner is harmless; no one who recognised the Roman rule as having authority *from above* could be

engaged in a serious rebellion; so *from that time Pilate
was seeking to release him*. But the Jews are implacable.
The word which is here translated *shouted aloud* means
" yelled " or " screamed "; but in English this seems
to be out of harmony with the dignity of the narrative.
(It is the same word in verse 6 and in xviii, 40.) Their
shout this time is to terrify: *If thou release this man,
thou art not a friend of Caesar*. Pilate's office entirely
depended on the favour of Tiberius; a report sent to
Rome that he had released a claimant to the throne
of Judea would be very dangerous to him; and he
could not deny either that *everyone who maketh himself
a king speaketh against Caesar* or that the Prisoner had
admitted that in some sense he claimed to be a king
(xviii, 36, 37). If he reported on his own behalf what
the Prisoner had actually said to him, this would seem
too preposterous to be even plausible.

So Pilate, *having heard these words*, establishes his
court for the first time. Everything hitherto has been
preliminary. He takes his seat upon a chair placed
for him on the dais of mosaic pavement, according to
custom; Julius Caesar is said to have carried about a
tessellated pavement to be set down wherever he
encamped, so that from it he could deliver judgements.
At this moment, when the formal trial before the
Governor takes place, St. John gives a note of date
and hour: the day was that of Preparation, or as we
might say " Friday of Passover week ". Preparation
is the name of the day before the Sabbath, that is,
Friday; *and it was about the sixth hour*. Does this
mean 6 A.M. or noon? Westcott gives sufficient reason
for thinking that St. John is following the use of
Asia Minor, where he was writing, in reckoning the
hours from midnight, not (as was the Jewish custom)
from 6 A.M. If so, the formal trial and sentence took
place at 6 A.M. and it was possible for the Crucifixion
itself to begin, as St. Mark tells us (xv, 25) at 9 A.M.
(" the third hour "). As it was about 3 A.M. when the

M

chief priests brought Jesus from the Sanhedrin to Pilate, there was plenty of time for the preliminary enquiry and Pilate's movements in and out of his palace before 6 A.M.

Pilate is yielding to the clamour of the Jews; but he will shew his scorn of them, and he will extract their profession of loyalty. He presents Jesus again to them: *Behold, your king.* Here is the man they present as a leader of revolt; well, perhaps He is a fitting king for such folk! The sight of the Lord calls forth a fresh outcry: *Away with him, away with him, crucify him.* Pilate presses his sarcasm home upon them: *Your king — shall I crucify him?* Now he hears what he has been waiting for. *The chief priests* — the official representatives of the Jewish theocracy — *answered "We have not a king except Caesar".*

He has humiliated these priests by forcing them to proclaim their loyalty to Caesar; so now he yields his Prisoner to them, so that the fury of the mob may be appeased and he himself escape the danger of a damaging report to Tiberius: *So then he delivered him to them to be crucified.*

*

(4) THE CRUCIFIXION (17-37)

(a) The Title (17-22)

So they received Jesus; and bearing the cross for himself he went forth to the place called the place of a Skull, which is called in Hebrew Golgotha, where they crucified him and with him two others on this side and on that, and in the midst Jesus. And Pilate wrote a title also and put it on the cross; and it was written " Jesus of Nazareth the King of the Jews". This title therefore read many of the Jews, because the place where Jesus was crucified was nigh to the city; and it was written in Hebrew, in Latin, and in Greek. The chief priests of the Jews therefore began to say to Pilate " Do not write ' The King of the Jews ' but that he said ' I am King of the Jews ' ". Pilate answered " What I have written, I have written ".

They received Jesus from the hands of Pilate, who has given the sentence, but leaves them to see to its

execution. The Lord goes forth *bearing the cross for
himself*. Later he would sink under its weight and
they would make Simon of Cyrene bear it after Him
(*St. Mark* xv, 21). He bore it for Himself; when we
turn to the spiritual load which it represents, we know
that none other can bear this; only God can bear it.
And even for Him it seems too great. We must ever
keep in mind the two thoughts — God the Creator of
the universe, which came into being at His word; God
the Redeemer staggering beneath a load that crushes
Him as He goes from Jerusalem to Calvary: so far
harder is it to redeem men from selfishness to love than
to create the wheeling systems of the stars. (And Simon
of Cyrene — the one African figure in the Gospels:
how true it is that Africa has been compelled to carry
the burden of a whole world's sin!)

And with him two others. Three crosses were set up
that day, and one or other we must accept for ourselves. One is the cross of the sinless Redeemer, which
cannot be ours. The others are the crosses of impeni-
tence and penitence; between those two we may,
indeed we must, make our choice.

St. John does not tell us that the *two others* were
thieves; we know, of course, that they must be condemned criminals; it is at least likely that they were
followers of Barabbas and that one of them brooded on
the difference between the leader whom he had followed
in a worldly insurrection and this other leader who
also is condemned because He claims a Kingdom (*St.
Luke* xxiii, 42).

That he was condemned on that ground is made
plain by the title which Pilate wrote and put on the
cross. Pilate did not miss this further opportunity to
shew his contempt for the Jews. He now treats Jesus
as having been what alone would justify the Jews in
demanding, or himself in pronouncing, the death-
sentence. If he was a merely idle claimant there
was no need to kill Him; let the chief priests suffer

the shame of the implication that there had been an ineffectual rising against the hated but irresistible power of Rome. When they begin to protest Pilate cuts them short with a snub; he will not change what he has written to please them.

So the Lord was *lifted up* (xii, 32) and began to " draw the nations nigh ". His reign is inaugurated. He is mounted on His throne of shame and power, the crown of glory and thorns is on His brow; and over His head is His title — the King of Israel, the King in the Kingdom of God. For so it was necessary that the Kingdom should be founded, since it must control the hearts and wills of men. " The Son of Man must suffer." He reigns from the Tree.

*

(b) The Distribution of Garments (23, 24)

The soldiers therefore, when they crucified Jesus, took his garments and made four parts, to each soldier a part — and his coat. But the coat was seamless, woven from the top throughout. They said therefore to one another " Let us not tear it but cast lots for it, whose it shall be "; that the scripture might be fulfilled " They parted my garments among themselves and upon my vesture they cast lots ". The soldiers therefore did these things.

It was a recognised custom that the soldiers who carried out an execution should take the clothes of the condemned prisoner as perquisites. As usual, a quaternion was charged with the duty of execution, so they make four piles of the other garments, but decide to cast lots for the seamless coat. That the coat is such is an illustration of the simplicity of the Lord's attire; His " coat " was a one-piece garment. But to the Evangelist it probably recalled the seamless coat of the High Priest, and was felt to be appropriate to Him who offered Himself as the one perfect sacrifice and atonement. Certainly he sees in the behaviour of the soldiers a fulfilment of Psalm xxii, 18, so that even

the conduct of the soldiers is part of the divine purpose
which is being at once revealed and accomplished.

*

(c) Three Words of the Crucified (25-30)

25-27. And there were standing by the Cross of Jesus his mother and
the sister of his mother, Mary the wife of Clopas and Mary Magdalene. Jesus therefore seeing his mother and the disciple standing by
whom he loved, saith to his mother " Woman; behold, thy son!"
Then saith he to the disciple " Behold, thy mother ". And from
that hour the disciple took her to his own home.

There were four women by the Cross — Mary the
Mother of the Lord and her sister, Salome, the mother
of the Beloved Disciple; also Mary the wife of Clopas
(brother, according to Hegesippus, of St. Joseph) and
Mary Magdalene; and among them was the Beloved
Disciple, the son of Salome, the nephew of the Blessed
Virgin and cousin of the Lord.

As the Lord looks down from the Cross He sees
this group of intimately dear friends. Especially He
sees His mother and knows how truly the prophecy of
Simeon is finding fulfilment — " a sword shall pierce
through thine own soul " (*St. Luke* ii, 35). Also He
knows that His own deepest agony is approaching —
the agony which, as it passes away to be succeeded by
the calm of achievement and trust, will find expression
in the words of the Psalmist " My God, my God, why
didst thou forsake me? " (*St. Mark* xv, 34). He would
not have His mother witness that agony. He com-
mends her to the care of her own nephew who is His
closest friend. And that disciple at once leads her
away from the scene of suffering. While he is absent
the period of darkness comes and passes; he returns
to hear the last words and to see the wondrous end.

*

28, 29. After this Jesus knowing that all things are now finished, that
the scripture might be accomplished, saith " I thirst ". A vessel

was set there full of vinegar; so they filled a sponge with the vinegar and, putting it on a javelin, lifted it to his mouth. When therefore he received the vinegar Jesus said " It is finished " and having bowed his head he gave up his spirit.

After this; the phrase does not mean that the later episode followed the earlier immediately, but only that it was later. In fact it was, no doubt, after the return of the Beloved Disciple, and therefore at least three hours later than the previous Word. The Lord knows that *all things are now finished*, as He will Himself proclaim very shortly (30). But He cannot make that proclamation till His parched throat is cooled and moistened. So He says " *I thirst* ", and in this again the Evangelist sees a fulfilment — indeed he calls it an accomplishment — of scripture, for the Psalmist had written " When I was thirsty they gave me vinegar to drink " (*Psalm* lxix, 21): but this reference is in the mind of the Evangelist rather than of the Lord Himself.

This Word *I thirst* is the only one of the seven which refers to the physical pain, and this is mentioned only to prepare for the great cry that follows. How impressive that though the pain of body was so great there was only this incidental allusion to it! Nor can we doubt that the very words *I thirst* carried with them for the Lord a recollection of the Cup that He had once prayed might pass from Him. He has accepted it with calm resolve; *the cup which My Father has given me, am I not to drink it?* (xviii, 11). Now He is eager to drink it to the dregs that all may be finished — *I thirst*.

Some kindly soldiers act in response; the *vinegar* or sour wine was there for the soldiers who had to keep watch. One or more of them *filled a sponge and, putting it on a javelin, lifted it to his mouth*. The true reading here is preserved in an ordinarily unimportant manuscript (the eleventh-century cursive, 476); if the sponge were attached to " hyssop ",[1] some rod or

---

[1] Hyssop is a plant which does not supply a strong stem, but does supply a bunch of leaves suitable for use as a " sprinkler ": cf. Exodus xii, 22.

pole would still be needed to lift it. But the corruption which led to this reading is easily understood, and we need not hesitate to follow the one manuscript which tells us that a javelin was used (see Bernard *ad loc.*).

When therefore he had received the vinegar — as soon as the parching thirst of His throat was allayed — *Jesus said " It is finished ".*

He knew *that all things were now finished* and He proclaims it to the world. This word was spoken " with a loud voice " (*St. Mark* xv, 37; *St. Matthew* xxvii, 50; *St. Luke* xxiii, 46). Each of the three Synoptists records that mighty cry; only St. John tells us what word was uttered. *It is finished*. All that prophets had foretold; all that the Father had sent Him to do (xvii, 4); the power of sin broken; the world overcome (xvi, 33); " *It is finished* ".

And having bowed his head, he gave up his spirit. So St. John refers to the words whispered with bowed head: " Father, into thy hands I commend my spirit " (*St. Luke* xxiii, 46). His death was a voluntary act; He had *authority to lay down* his life (x, 18), and He exercises that authority. His final act is to " give up " — of course to the Father — that spirit which was always *in the bosom of the Father* (i, 18). He goes His way to the Father (xvi, 10).

*

(*d*) The Spear-thrust (31-37)

The Jews therefore, since it was Preparation, that the bodies might not remain up on the cross on the sabbath, for the day of that sabbath was a great day, asked Pilate that their legs might be broken and that they might be taken away. The soldiers therefore came and brake the legs of the first and of the other who was crucified with him. But having come to Jesus, when they saw that he was already dead, they did not break his legs, but one of the soldiers with a spear pierced his side and forthwith came there out blood and water. And he who hath seen hath borne witness, and true is his witness, and he knoweth that he saith things that are true that ye also may believe. For these things came to pass that the scripture might be fulfilled " A bone of him shall not be broken "; and again another scripture saith " They shall look on him whom they pierced ".

The law forbids that criminals should remain on the cross after sunset (*Deuteronomy* xxi, 23); and this was specially urgent if at that sunset the Sabbath began so that another twenty-four hours must elapse before they could be buried; if the Sabbath were the *great day* of a feast the urgency was all the greater. But the Roman custom, while burial on the same day was not forbidden, was to leave the corpse on the cross as a deterrent to others. So Pilate's leave was necessary. He had not wanted to condemn Jesus to death; nor can he want trouble when the pilgrims flock into the city for the feast; so his consent is readily given. The customary way of ending the life of crucified criminals was the cruel one of breaking their legs with a heavy mallet, when the shock would cause the death which exhaustion had brought near. The soldiers break the legs of the other two, whom we must therefore suppose to be still alive at the time; but they find Jesus already dead. One of them, perhaps to make doubly sure, thrusts a spear into His side. *And forthwith came there out blood and water.*

The Evangelist attaches great importance to this strange event. He seems to regard it as in some way a sign that the Lord, though truly dead, is yet also alive. Probably also he thinks of the blood as the Blood of the New Covenant, shed upon the Cross but also given and received in the Eucharist, and of the water as the symbol of spiritual life (iv, 14; vii, 37-39) and the cleansing element of Baptism; so that from the sacrifice of the Cross flows the grace of the two great sacraments.

The Evangelist is careful to insist that his record rests on the testimony of an eyewitness — *he who hath seen hath borne witness*; that this testimony is reliable — *and true is his witness*; and that the eyewitness him-

self, the Beloved Disciple (who must therefore have
been still alive when the Elder wrote the Gospel)
knoweth that he saith things that are true; *that ye also* —
like that apostle — *may believe.*

Then the Evangelist adds his own tracing in these
events of the fulfilment of scripture, and consequent
new understanding of the events themselves. As the
seamless coat suggested the High Priest, so the
unbroken bones suggest the Paschal Lamb (*Exodus* xii,
46); He is Himself both Priest and Victim. The
other reference carries us forward; for the words of
Zechariah (x, 12) " they shall look unto Him whom
they have pierced ", speak of a repentance of Jerusalem
for the killing of that " good shepherd whom her
people have rejected and slain ".[1] Thus the present
episode points to the time when the Lord on His Cross
shall indeed draw all men unto Him, even those who
nailed Him there—even us who crucify Him afresh.

*

(5) THE BURIAL (38-42)

And after these things Joseph of Arimathea, being a disciple of Jesus,
but secretly for fear of the Jews, asked Pilate that he might take
away the body of Jesus. And Pilate gave leave. He came therefore and took his body. And there came also Nicodemus, who came
to him by night at the first, bringing a mixture of myrrh and aloes,
about a hundred pounds. So they took the body of Jesus and wound
it in linen clothes with the spices, as is the custom for the Jews to
bury. And there was, in the place where he was crucified, a garden,
and in the garden a new tomb, in which no one had yet been laid.
There, therefore, because of the Jews' Preparation, because the
tomb was near, they laid Jesus.

Joseph of Arimathea was a timid disciple, like most
of us. But he could not bear that the body of the Lord
should be dishonoured. As with many timid natures,
a strong and deep sentiment prevailed where the call
of truth was insufficient. He " plucked up his courage "

---

1 George Adam Smith, *The Book of the Twelve Prophets*, p. 482.

(*St. Mark* xv, 43) and begged Pilate for the charge of the body. His request was granted, and he superintended the taking down of the body from the Cross (*St. Mark* xv, 46). His courage gave courage to another similarly placed, so that the last rites were rendered by two men who had never dared to avow themselves disciples. Yet perhaps it was for that very reason that they were able now to shew the care and reverence for which all Christians thank them. It would seem that this burial was regarded as provisional, as it was certainly hurried. It was the impending Sabbath which caused the haste. So that Sabbath law which was the first occasion of a conspiracy to kill the Lord (v. 18) determined the manner of His burial.

Had the old system and the power of darkness triumphed?

ACT V

THE DAWN

CHAPTER XX

THE conflict of Light with Darkness is finished. For a moment Darkness seemed to prevail: " this is your hour and the power of darkness " (*St. Luke* xxii, 53). But the fight was fought out and the victory won: *It is finished* (xix, 30). The date of the triumph of love is Good Friday, not Easter Day. Yet if the story had ended there, the victory would have been barren. What remains is not to win it, but to gather in its fruits. Consequently St. John does not present the Resurrection as a mighty act by which the hosts of evil are routed, but rather as the quiet rising of the sun which has already vanquished night. The atmosphere of the story has all the sweet freshness of dawn on a spring day. Fra Angelico, in his delicious *fresco* of the appearance of the Lord to Mary Magdalene, has perfectly caught its tone and feeling.

The story is told, and the Appearances selected, so as to illustrate, as Westcott says, " the passage from sight to faith ". The Beloved Disciple believes when he sees the grave-clothes; Mary Magdalene when she hears a well-known voice pronounce her name; the ten apostles when they see the Lord's wounds; St. Thomas when he sees those same wounds and is invited to handle them. But better than all of these is a faith that needs no such support from experiences of the senses (29). All the Appearances, as we shall see, give emphasis to what had been said: " *It is expedient for you that I go away. For if I go not away, the Comforter will not come to you, but if I depart I will send him to you* (xvi, 7). Mary is to cling to the ascended Lord, not to the Master who addresses her with physical speech; the Apostles are to receive Christ's own life-breath or spirit to be their spirit and the breath of

their lives; Thomas, who reaches the first confession
of full Christian faith, is pointed to an apprehension of
divine truth which is independent of all external
evidence. The Lord is calling His followers to enter
on the transition " from sight to faith" — from outward companionship to inward communion, from the
discipleship which rests on a bodily Presence to one
which is perfected in spiritual union — " *I in them,
and thou in me* " (xvii, 23; cf. xiv, 20).

*

(1) THE EMPTY TOMB

But on the first day of the week Mary Magdalene cometh early, while
it was still dark, to the tomb, and seeth the stone taken away out of
the tomb. So she runneth and cometh to Simon Peter, and to the
other disciple whom Jesus loved, and saith to them " They took the
Lord out of the tomb and we do not know where they put him ".
So Peter set out and the other disciple; and they were coming to
the tomb; and they began to run, the two of them together; and the
other disciple ran on in front, quicker than Peter, and came first to
the tomb and, peeping in, seeth lying there the linen clothes, yet he
did not go in. So Simon Peter cometh also, following him, and
went into the tomb; and he taketh note of the linen clothes lying,
and the napkin, which was on his head, not lying with the linen
clothes but apart, wrapped into one place. So then the other
disciple also went in — he who came first to the tomb — and saw
and believed. For not yet did they know the scripture, that he
must rise from the dead. So the disciples went away again to their
own homes.

It is most manifestly the record of a personal
memory. Nothing else can account for the little details,
so vivid, so little like the kind of thing that comes
from invention or imagination.

*On the first day of the week Mary Magdalene cometh
early.* She who is supremely the forgiven sinner,
whose heart is utterly given to her Saviour, is the first
to go, when the Sabbath is over, to be near by that
Body of which she has twice already anointed the feet,
and to which she would now aid in giving the last

care of love (*St. Luke* vii, 36-50; *St. John* xii, 1-8;
St. Mark xvi, 1). Perhaps she came with the other
devoted women; but if so St. John's narrative suggests
that she was before them. She comes *early* — that is
to say, soon after 3 A.M. (see xviii, 28) — *while it was
still dark*. But the dawn is already breaking, and she
can see that something has happened; the mouth of
the tomb, which had been closed by a great stone, is
open ; *she seeth the stone taken away out of the tomb*. She
does not look further; she jumps to two conclusions —
first that the Body of the Lord is no longer in the tomb,
and secondly that this is because His enemies have
stolen it. At once she turns and *runneth and cometh to
Simon Peter, and to the other disciple whom Jesus loved,
and saith to them " They took the Lord out of the tomb
and we do not know where they put him "*. She runs
first to Peter, who, in spite of his denials, is still thought
of as the leader, and to that other disciple who was
known as the most intimate; the Greek phrasing
makes it clear that they were not together and she
had to run on a separate errand to each. Her message
is not what she had seen, but the inference she had
drawn; in her dismay she is so sure that she states it
as a definite fact: *they took* — in English it would
be *they came and took the Lord out of the tomb and we do
not know where they put him*. This loving woman, who
had anointed and kissed the feet of the Lord, identifies
Him with His Body. To remove that is to remove
Him; and she does not know how to shew Him
reverence.

There follows a very vivid description of the two
disciples hurrying to the tomb. They set forth at
once; as they approach the tomb they begin to
run; the younger, John, gains on his comrade and
reaches the tomb first. *So Peter set out, and the other
disciple; and they were coming to the tomb; and they
began to run, the two of them together; and the other
disciple ran on in front quicker than Peter, and came first*

to the tomb, and, peeping in, seeth lying there the linen clothes; yet he did not go in. The Beloved Disciple is the first to reach the tomb; but he can at first do no more than *peep in* — for this was at the date of the Gospel's writing the common meaning of the Greek word here used; a sacred awe of the Lord's burial-place holds him outside. But he sees what later he will recognise as most significant — *lying there the linen clothes.* The eager and impulsive Simon Peter is not content to stand outside. *So Simon Peter cometh also, following him, and went into the tomb.* He not only *seeth* the linen clothes, but carefully observes them: *he taketh note of the linen clothes lying, and the napkin, which was on his head, not lying with the linen clothes, but apart, wrapped into one place.* The Body of the Lord had, as it would seem, passed through the winding-sheets that were about it, so that these lay there, the upper layer having fallen upon the lower; more significant still, *the napkin which was on his head* had similarly fallen in upon itself and lay there, *apart* — separated by the brief space where the neck had been — *wrapped* or *heaped into one place.* It is extraordinarily vivid, and such as no invention would devise, no freak of imagination conjure up. Peter does not see the significance. " Peter . . . seeth the linen clothes by themselves; and went away to his home wondering at that which was come to pass " (*St. Luke* xxiv, 12).

Then the Beloved Disciple, taking courage from Peter, goes into the tomb; he saw what Peter had seen; but he grasps its meaning. *So then the other disciple also went in* — *he who came first to the tomb* — *and saw and believed.* Perhaps he who was in heart nearest to the Lord had some instinct of understanding which enabled him to interpret what he saw and grasp the truth; anyhow, the " disciple whom Jesus loved " was the first to believe in His resurrection.

The Evangelist adds a note to explain how it was that the apostles needed to reach that belief by gradual stages. *For not yet did they know the scripture, that he must rise from the dead.* They had not learnt to apply to their Lord, as Peter would a few weeks later, the great declaration of the Psalmist: " Thou wilt not leave my soul to Sheol; neither wilt thou suffer thy holy one to see corruption " (*Psalm* xvi, 11; *Acts* ii, 27). But for the disciple whose heart was uplifted by faith there was no more to see or to do at the tomb than for the disciple whose heart was full of bewilderment. *So the disciples went away again to their own homes.*

*

(2) THE APPEARANCE TO MARY MAGDALENE

But there was one who could not leave the tomb. Mary Magdalene, having taken her despairing message to Peter and John, had returned to the tomb, and lingered there. Even though the Lord had been taken away, it was here that He had been laid; this is the place of latest association with him.

11-18. But Mary stood by the tomb without, weeping. So as she wept, she peeped into the tomb; and she noticeth two angels in white sitting one by the head and one by the feet where had lain the body of Jesus. And they say to her " Woman, why art thou weeping? " She saith to them " They took my Lord and I do not know where they put him ". Having said this she turned backwards and noticeth Jesus standing, and did not know that it was Jesus. Jesus saith to her " Woman, why art thou weeping? For whom art thou looking? " She, thinking that it is the gardener, saith to him, " Sir, if it was thou that carried him away, tell me where thou didst put him and I will take him ". Jesus saith to her " Mary ". She turned and saith to him in Hebrew " Rabboni " (which means Master). Jesus saith to her " Cling not to me, for not yet am I gone up to the Father. But go to my brethren and say to them — I go up to my Father and your Father, and my God and your God." Mary Magdalene cometh announcing to the disciples " I have seen the Lord " and that he said these things to her.

Mary remains at the tomb in tears; so she had wept at the tomb of her brother, Lazarus (xi, 31). Gradually

N

her sorrow becomes tinged with wonder what it was that the two apostles had seen when they went into the tomb; so she too looks in, peeping as John had peeped at first. What catches her attention is not the linen clothes, but *two angels in white sitting one by the head and one by the feet where had lain the body of Jesus.* The place of His death was between two thieves; "He was numbered with the transgressors" (*Isaiah* liii, 12; *St. Luke* xxii, 37). The place of His burial was between two angels; for God had set Him forth in His blood to be a mercy-seat — the place where God's forgiveness meets man's sin (*Romans* iii, 25).

We do ill to ask whether there was one angel (*St. Mark* xvi, 16) or two (*St. Luke* xxiv, 4). It is not to be presumed that angels are physical objects reflecting rays of light upon the retina of the eye. When men "see" or "hear" angels, it is rather to be supposed that an intense interior awareness of a divine message leads to the projection of an image which is then experienced as an occasion of something seen and heard. That divine messengers were sent and divine messages received we need not doubt; that they took physical form so that all who "saw" anything must "see" the same thing we need not suppose. Here they are the manifestation to Mary that God was intimately active in this strange matter of the empty tomb, and was active also to comfort the sorrow of her heart. The divine consolation approaches her tenderly; the angels ask only why she is weeping. Her answer is to repeat the message of dismay which she had brought to the two disciples; but she repeats it with two little variations; now it is not "the Lord" but "my Lord" — not "we do not know" but "I do not know". For when she first came and found the stone removed (1) she came in company with the other women or had soon been joined by them (*St. Mark* xvi, 1). But now she is alone: *They took my Lord and I do not know where they put him.*

As she says this, the sorrow comes upon her again in its first fulness, and she turns away from the tomb and its angels. She notices someone standing there; but she does not recognise Him; probably she does not look up at Him; no doubt it is someone who has his own business there. *She turned backward and noticeth Jesus standing, and did not know that it was Jesus.* He too begins, as the angels had begun, by asking the cause of her grief — the first step towards ordinary sympathy: *Woman, why art thou weeping?* But He knows the real answer, so He adds words which shew His understanding. *For whom art thou looking?* She still does not look up or straight towards Him; speaking with downcast face and looking away to hide her tears, supposing that He is the gardener she says, *Sir, if it was thou that carried him away, tell me where thou didst put him and I will take him.* The word for " carried away " has a suggestion of stealing (xii, 6), but here contains no more than a sad complaint, not a charge. Mary does not answer the question, nor indicate in any way of whom she speaks. That, in her absorption in her grief, seems to her manifest. Her one desire is to find the Lord's Body and take it where friends will pay to it the last tribute of love and honour.

Mary: the answer is her own name, spoken by a voice she knew. The earlier questions, though spoken by that voice, could not recall the old association. Her name, so spoken, reaches her heart. She turns to face the Speaker. *Rabboni:* the cry of devotion accompanies a movement as she hastens to clasp those feet which once she had bathed with tears. So she draws the first declaration of the Risen Christ. *Cling not to me, for not yet am I gone up to the Father.* The weakness to which such love as Mary's is liable is that it clings too closely to the physical form, of which the whole purpose is to express and serve the spiritual self. To her therefore this warning is appropriately given, but its meaning is for all. She must learn to love and trust and serve, even though she can no longer caress His feet or hear His voice pronounce her name. Not to the Lord as He tabernacled in the flesh, subject to all limitations of the body, is she to cling ; but to the Lord in His perfect union with the Father.

So He taught her the meaning of that last Appearance, the final withdrawal of His physical presence, which we call the Ascension. It was separation in one sense, for it closed the period of the first form of intercourse. But in a profounder sense it was the inauguration of a fuller union. In the days of His earthly ministry, only those could speak to Him who came where He was. If He was in Galilee, men could not find Him in Jerusalem; if He was in Jerusalem, men could not find Him in Galilee. But His Ascension means that He is perfectly united with God; we are with Him wherever we are present to God; and that is everywhere and always. Because He is " in Heaven " He is everywhere on earth; because He is ascended, He is here now. Our devotion is not to hold us by the empty tomb; it must lift up our hearts to heaven so that we too " in heart and mind thither ascend and with Him continually dwell " ; it must also send us forth into the world to do His will; and these are not two things, but one.

Not yet am I gone up to the Father. To use the word " ascended " is to introduce a specialised term where a quite general one is found in the Greek. He had spoken of Himself as *coming down out of heaven* (vi, 38), and had balanced this by speaking of His *going up where he was before* (vi, 62). He has repeatedly spoken of " going to the Father ". All this is here in mind. The essential moment of His going to the Father is the consummation of Love upon the Cross: *It is finished*. But He still subjects Himself to some measure of physical limitation that He may appear in His Risen

Body to the disciples and send them out to gather the fruits of His triumph. *Not yet* therefore is complete that " going " or " going up " to the Father, which is at once the climax of His earthly life, and the source of His disciples' power to do wonders in His Name (xiv, 12). Alike for fulness of our love to Him, and for fulness of His power working in us, we are to cling, not to the Lord known after the flesh (*II Corinthians* v, 16) but to the Lord enthroned at the right hand of the Father and active within us by the energy of His Holy Spirit.

Mary is to carry to the disciples the news of the imminent consummation; the message is expressed in language which emphasises communion rather than separation. *Go to my brethren* — a new title for the disciples due to the prominence of the thought that the Father is both His Father and ours; it is characteristic of the days after the Resurrection; see *St. Matthew* xxviii, 10, where also it is associated with direction to await the Ascension — *and say to them* — *I go up to my Father and your Father, and my God and your God.*

The command is at once obeyed. This forgiven sinner becomes the messenger of Christ to the Apostles themselves, declaring the Resurrection of her Lord and theirs. *Mary Magdalene cometh announcing to the disciples " I have seen the Lord" and that he said these things to her.*

*

FIRST APPEARANCE TO THE DISCIPLES

19-23. When therefore it was evening on that day, the first day of the week, and the doors having been shut where the disciples were on account of their fear of the Jews, came Jesus and stood in the midst, and saith to them " Peace to you ". And having said this he shewed both his hands and his side to them. Filled with joy therefore were the disciples on seeing the Lord. So Jesus said to them again " Peace to you. As the Father hath sent me, I also send you." And having said this he breathed upon them and saith to them " Receive holy spirit (or breath). If of any ye forgive the sins, they are forgiven them; if of any ye hold them fast, they are held."

When therefore it was evening on that day, — late in the evening, for the two disciples who had walked to Emmaus were returned (*St. Luke* xxiv, 29, 33-36) — *and the doors having been shut where the disciples were on account of their fear of the Jews,* for no doubt the story of the empty tomb was known and the disciples might well be charged with stealing the Body — *came Jesus and stood in the midst.* We need not say that He came through the closed doors; the Evangelist does not say that; the word *came* implies no more than that at one time He was not there and at a later time He was. But the story does imply that the Risen Body was free from some of its former limitations. He stood there among them, and spoke the familiar greeting *Peace to you.* It was a common salutation. But the disciples would recall the words: *Peace I leave to you, the peace that is mine I give to you. Not as the world gives do I give to you. Let not your hearts be troubled or dismayed* (xiv, 27). To confirm their conviction that it is He Himself, *having said this he shewed both his hands and his side to them.* It was proof of identity; this, however transmuted, was the Body which had hung on the Cross and was laid in the tomb. But the scars are more than this; they are the evidence not only that what they see is the Body of Jesus, but what is the quality for ever of the Body of Him whom they know with ever-deeper understanding as the Christ: " the Son of Man must suffer ".

The wounds of Christ are His credentials to the suffering race of men. Shortly after the end of the Great War, when its memories and its pains were fresh in mind, a volume was published under the title *Jesus of the Scars, and Other Poems* by Edward Shillito. The poem from which the title was taken stands first in the book and is headed by the text, " He showed them His hands and His side " :

If we have never sought, we seek Thee now;
  Thine eyes burn through the dark, our only stars;
We must have sight of thorn-pricks on Thy brow,
  We must have Thee, O Jesus of the Scars.

The heavens frighten us ; they are too calm;
  In all the universe we have no place.
Our wounds are hurting us ; where is the balm?
  Lord Jesus, by Thy Scars, we claim Thy grace.

If, when the doors are shut, Thou drawest near,
  Only reveal those hands, that side of Thine;
We know to-day what wounds are, have no fear,
  Show us Thy Scars, we know the countersign.

The other gods were strong; but Thou wast weak;
  They rode, but Thou didst stumble to a throne;
But to our wounds only God's wounds can speak,
  And not a god has wounds, but Thou alone.

Only a God in whose perfect Being pain has its place can win and hold our worship ; for otherwise the creature would in fortitude surpass the Creator.

Filled with joy therefore were the disciples on seeing the Lord. His promise was fulfilled: *I shall see you again, and your joy no man taketh from you* (xvi, 22). We imagine a few moments of silent rapture at this proof that their Lord is alive and that their fellowship with Him is renewed. Then He repeats His greeting and goes on to give the apostolic commission and at the same time to suggest the new form which must now be taken by the fellowship of the disciples with Himself: *Peace to you. As the Father hath sent me, I also send you.* Still the position of Mediator is asserted; the Father : the Son : : the Son : the Apostles. We are called to share His apostolic ministry; but no other among men, however inspired, becomes the equal of Christ; for His mission is from the Father without intermediary, and ours is from the Father through Him. But as there is need at times to check our sense of the dignity of our status, so it is impossible to exaggerate the greatness of our calling. It is to continue in the world that divine Mission of which the inauguration was the sending of the Son by the Father to be the Redeemer of the world. We are members of the Body of Christ, through whom He would accomplish His purpose. All accounts of the charge given to the disciples by the Risen Lord agree in its content; they were to go forth to be His witnesses (*St. Luke* xxiv, 47, 48; Acts i, 8), to proclaim the Gospel (*St. Mark* xvi, 15), to make disciples of all the nations (*St. Matthew* xxviii, 19), to continue the Mission of the Incarnation (*St. John* xx, 21). For this purpose they could rely on His presence (*St. Matthew* xxviii, 20) — the power of the Holy Spirit (Acts i, 8; *St. Luke* xxiv, 49; *St. John* xx, 21).

This is the primary purpose for which the Spirit is given : that we may bear witness to Christ. We must not expect the gift while we ignore the purpose. A Church which ceases to be missionary will not be, and cannot rightly expect to be, " spiritual ".

And having said this he breathed upon them and saith to them " Receive holy spirit (or *breath*). *If of any ye forgive the sins, they are forgiven them; if of any ye hold them fast, they are held."* The fellowship of the old days has for a moment been renewed, but only that it may give place to the new and still closer fellowship which is to last for ever. He imparts to them His own life-breath; the outward sign, helped by the play on words, suggests that henceforth His own spiritual energy will be within them. *Receive holy spirit.* The gift is freely offered, but it can be refused; there is a definite act of reception. The Lord now fulfils the promise of the Baptist concerning Him (i, 33); He baptises His disciples, not in water which washes away stains, but in holy spirit — the energy of a holy life in obedience to God.

Receive holy spirit — not " the Holy Spirit ". What is bestowed is not the Divine Person Himself but the

power and energy of which He is the source. Earlier
it had been said *not yet was there spirit, because Jesus
was not yet glorified* (vii, 39). But now that glorification is complete, and it is possible for the new divine
energy, which operates through man's response to the
manifested love of God, to begin its activity. Of this
the outstanding manifestation will be the continuance
of that divine offer of life which always (incidentally)
involves judgement (iii, 17–19). *If of any ye forgive
the sins, they are forgiven them; and if of any ye hold
them fast, they are held.* The body of disciples, being
the Body of Christ, and being filled with that holy
spirit which Christ has breathed into them, carries
forward His work of pronouncing God's forgiveness
of sin. The authority here bestowed is given to the
body, not, or at least not necessarily or certainly, to
any one member of that body; and it is given in connexion with the bestowal of holy spirit — the energy
and power of God the Holy Spirit in the fellowship
and in the heart. The principle is clear. To the
Church as the fellowship of the Spirit is given the
authority of Christ Himself as Pardoner and Judge.
But only so far as the Church in and through its
members fulfils the condition — *Receive holy spirit* —
can it discharge this function.

In practice the Church must do this through
appropriate organs, and the parallel charge to St.
Peter included in the Matthaean account of his confession at Caesarea Philippi (*St. Matthew* xvi, 19)
supports the practice of the Church in translating this
commission from the plural to the singular in the
Ordination of Priests. But

the fundamental Christian Ministry is the Ministry of Christ.
There is no Christian Priesthood or Ministry apart from
His. His priestly and ministerial function is to reconcile the
world to God in and through himself, by His Incarnation and
by His 'one sacrifice once offered', delivering men from the
power of sin and death.

The Church as the Body of Christ, sharing His life, has a ministerial function derived from that of Christ. In this function every member has his place and share according to his different capabilities and calling. The work of the Church is to bring all the various activities and relationships of men under the control of the Holy Spirit, and in this work each member has his part. The particular function of the official Ministry can only be rightly understood as seen against the background of this universal ministry.[1]

Every Christian has a responsibility for drawing others to Christ, and for declaring, if occasion so require, the forgiveness which the divine love offers to all who come in penitence. It is evidently appropriate that this, like other functions, should be representatively exercised by those appointed for the purpose; none the less the minister so appointed, when he pronounces absolution, does it, not in the name of his fellow-Christians, but in the name of Christ; for it is only in His name and by His commission that it can be pronounced at all.

If the gift of holy spirit has been fully and perfectly " received ", the individual Christian so endowed would have perfect discernment and his judgement in forgiving sins or " retaining " them would be that of God Himself. But only the Lord Himself was able to receive the gift of the Spirit in that fulness. The individual priest, who has been bidden at his Ordination to receive that gift, must do his best according to the measure in which he has in fact received it. The Church, for its temporal purposes, must act as though the judgement of the priest were that of God, and must warn a sinner who has been judged impenitent and to whom absolution has been refused, not to share in the Holy Communion. But the Church does not suppose that its ministers are infallible, or declare that one who is excluded from the Christian fellowship on earth is certainly excluded from the fellowship of

[1] *Doctrine in the Church of England* (The Report of the Archbishops' Commission on Doctrine), p. 114.

Christ in Heaven. And the priest, though he rightly warns those who approach him that they need to " receive " the benefit of absolution, and that this is only possible so far as their penitence is real, will not so far trust his own " reception " of the gift of the Spirit as to refuse to pronounce absolution unless the lack of penitence is very evident. For the ministry which he has received is not essentially a ministry of judgement; it is essentially a ministry of reconciliation, and of judgement only incidentally, to those who refuse to be reconciled.

*

The Appearance to Thomas

24–29. But Thomas, one of the Twelve, called Didymus, was not with them when Jesus came. So the other disciples began to say to him " We have seen the Lord ". But he said to them, " Unless I see in his hands the print of the nails and put my finger into the print of the nails, and put my hand into his side, I shall in nowise believe ". And after eight days again his disciples were within and Thomas with them. Jesus cometh, the doors having been shut, and stood in the midst and said " Peace to you ". Then he saith to Thomas " Bring hither thy finger and see my hands; and bring thy hand and put it into my side, and do not become unbelieving but believing ". Thomas answered and said to him " My Lord and my God ". Jesus saith to him " Is it because thou hast seen me that thou hast believed ? Blessed are they who saw not and have believed."

So doubting Thomas receives the " sign " which was refused to enquiring Pharisees — e.g. *St. Mark* viii, 11, 12. Why are they differently treated? Of course it is because the Pharisees did not want to believe, and if they had been convinced by a " sign from heaven" they would have been unwilling adherents, not truly disciples at all. To give them the sign would be to yield to the temptation typified by the throwing of Himself down from the pinnacle of the Temple. Their demand proceeded from ill-will; it was necessary first to cure that ill-will. Nothing can be more remote from discipleship than a man who should suppose the Gospel to be true while wishing that it were not.

The doubt of Thomas, on the other hand, proceeded from loyalty and good-will. He was utterly devoted. It was he who had said *let us also go that we may die with him* (xi, 16). But he was rather literal-minded; it was he who said *We know not whither thou goest: how know we the way?* (xiv, 5). He could not dare to believe the tremendous news; and, after all, the other disciples were equally unable to believe at first (*St. Luke* xxiv, 11). He was not present when on the evening of the first Easter Day the Lord appeared to the ten apostles and, perhaps, to other disciples assembled with them; and when they tell him, he still refuses to believe. It is natural to the prosaic temperament to demand certainty as a condition of self-commital. His negative is very strong: *unless I see in his hands the print of the nails and put my finger into the print of the nails, and put my hand into his side, I shall in nowise believe* — or — *there is no chance of my believing.* Such vigour of disbelief plainly represents a strong urge to believe, held down by common sense and its habitual dread of disillusionment.

The Lord waits till all the associations of the earlier scene can again be present. Again it is the first day of the week — the resurrection-day. Again the disciples are assembled behind closed doors. Again the Lord suddenly stands in the midst with His salutation *Peace to you*. Then at once He turns to Thomas and shews His knowledge of His disciple's heart. Thomas is offered precisely the test which he had demanded; but he does not avail himself of it. He does not touch the marks of the wounds; but at once he leaps to the first confession of true Christian faith: *My Lord and my God*.

The disciples could not maintain themselves at that level. The full doctrine of the Deity of Jesus is not apparent in the speeches recorded in Acts. But

St. Stephen grasped this truth devotionally, when he commended his spirit to the Lord Jesus as to God (*Acts* vii, 59); and there was, apparently, no sense that St. Paul was departing from the original Gospel as he developed his Christology. The Church of Jerusalem was perplexed and troubled about him in many ways, but not in this. Gradually we watch the Church moving towards a well-grounded assurance of that truth which St. Thomas reached in the exaltation of his sudden deliverance from obstinate gloom to radiant faith.

Do not become unbelieving but believing. He was not an unbeliever, in the sense of distrusting the Lord who had been his Master. But he was on the way to this through his fixed refusal to believe the new revelation of that Lord. Let him reverse the process of his mind, and instead of moving towards unbelief, move towards full belief.

And so he did. But he must not be left to suppose that the real cause of his new and full belief is the granting of his desire for a test, even to the limited extent to which he had availed himself of what was offered. He had demanded sight and touch; the Lord has offered Himself to both; Thomas does not seek to touch. He has seen; that is enough. But that is not the real cause of his belief, any more than a similar wonder had been the cause of Nathanael's belief long ago (i, 50): *Is it because thou hast seen me that thou hast believed?* Do you really suppose that the ground of your faith is your experience in this moment? No; of course not; it is grounded in that loyalty which made you ready to share your Master's journey to death. This moment has done no more than release a faith which was ready, if it could find an occasion, to burst its inhibitions.

Yet it is true that the most blessed state is that of a faith which has no inhibitions to burst through. Just as it is best to believe that Christ is in the Father and the Father in Him by a direct apprehension of the Deity manifest in Him, whereas to believe *for the works' sake* is a second-best (xiv, 11), so it is most blessed to be able to believe in His Deity and triumph over death by direct apprehension, because as we dwell with Him we behold His glory: *blessed are they who saw not and have believed.*

St. Peter wrote to Christians who, like ourselves, had had no opportunity to see the Lord, and used the expression "Whom, not having seen, ye love; on whom, though now ye see him not, yet believing, ye rejoice greatly with joy unspeakable and full of glory" (*I Peter* i. 8). We have not seen. Do we believe? Do we love? Can we claim the blessing — the "joy unspeakable and full of glory"?

*

THE CONCLUSION

30-31. Many other signs truly did Jesus in the presence of the disciples, which have not been written in this book. But these have been written that ye may believe that Jesus is the Christ, the Son of God, and that believing ye may have Life in his name.

St. John has not attempted to give a complete account of the Lord's life. There was much that He did which His disciples saw, and much of this had been already recorded. (The Fourth Evangelist was certainly familiar with our Second and Third Gospels.) And nearly everything He did was a "sign"; that is to say, it was an expression of a spiritual truth or power, to which it pointed. Among all the acts that might be recorded, St. John has chosen those which are written in his book, in order that we may find in them what he has found: *that ye may believe that Jesus is the Christ, the Son of God, and that believing ye may have Life in his name.*

That Jesus is the Christ, the Son of God. Peter reached this belief at Caesarea Philippi; Martha con-

fesses it before the restoration of Lazarus to life
(xi, 27). But the words mean more now; for men have
" crucified the Lord of glory ", and if we preach Christ
Jesus as Lord, we preach a Christ on a cross (*I
Corinthians* ii, 8; *II Corinthians* iv, 5; *I Corinthians* i,
23). We are to believe that the Kingdom of God was
inaugurated — for this is the function of the Christ
— by the Life and Death and Resurrection of Jesus;
we are to believe that He is the Son of God, in whom
we see the Father.

Believe and have life. The two go together. " He
that hath the Son hath the Life; he that hath not the
Son of God hath not the Life. These things have I
written unto you, that ye may know that ye have
eternal Life, even unto you that believe on the name
of the Son of God " (*I John* v, 12, 13). Indeed Life
does not so much result from, but rather consists in
the knowledge of God in His Son: *this is the eternal
Life, to know thee the only true God, and whom thou
sendedst — Jesus Christ* (xvii, 3).

We are to have this Life *in his name* — in His
manifested nature and character. There we find it;
abiding there we enjoy it.

" This is the true God and eternal Life. Little
children, guard yourselves from idols " (*I John* v, 21).

EPILOGUE

CHAPTER XXI

The Gospel as originally planned is now ended, and the motive of its composition has been stated: *that ye may believe that Jesus is the Christ, the Son of God, and that believing ye may have Life in his name* (xx, 31).

Yet to end there would be in a very real sense misleading. For the work of the Lord, which is at once the ground of faith in Him and the vindication of that faith, was in one sense incomplete. The victory was won; but its fruits had still to be gathered. In respect of what the Lord actually accomplishes in the souls of men, the narrative of His earthly ministry can be no more than the record of " all that Jesus *began* both to do and to teach, until the day in which he was received up " (*Acts* i, 1). The *Book of the Acts of the Apostles* and the subsequent history of the Church tell us what Jesus went on, and goes on, both to do and to teach after the day in which He was received up. To complete the Gospel itself there is need of an indication of the principles of the Lord's activity in His Body, the Church; this is now given in two narratives, of which the former speaks of the condition on which alone the work of disciples is effectual (1-14), while the latter speaks of the condition on which alone the commission to work for Christ is given (15-22).

At the same time the opportunity is taken to answer two questions which were causing perplexity to that generation for which the Gospel was originally written. The first of these concerned the position in the Church occupied by St. Peter from the earliest days after the Ascension (*Acts* i, 15, etc.); the other concerned the apparent probability that the Lord's Coming would not take place until the last of the Apostolic band was already dead, though He Himself

397   O 2

had said, " There be some here of them that stand by, which shall in no wise taste of death, till they see the kingdom of God come with power " (*St. Mark* ix, 1). The Kingdom of God did come with power in and through the Crucifixion (see Introduction, pp. xxix-xxxi). But this had not been understood. When all the Apostles were dead except the Beloved Disciple, it was natural to connect this saying with him, and to suppose that to him it had been promised that he should not die till the final consummation; and the words used to St. Peter with a very different purpose were misinterpreted in this sense. It was important to fend off the disappointment that would arise when the Beloved Disciple died and the end was not yet.

*

(1) The Lord and the Body of Disciples (1-14)

(a) The Work of the Disciples (1-11)

(i) *At their own Pleasure*

1-3. After these things Jesus manifested himself again to the disciples by the sea of Tiberias; and he did it in this way. There were together Simon Peter, and Thomas who is called the Twin, Nathanael from Cana of Galilee, and the sons of Zebedee and other of his disciples two. Then saith to them Simon Peter " I am going off to fish ". They say to him " We too are coming with thee ". So they went out and got into the boat; and in that night they caught nothing.

In spite of the great experiences recorded in Chapter XX the disciples have not yet found the new direction for their lives. They are returned to Galilee. The only change from the old days, before ever they heard the Baptist say, " Behold, the Lamb of God " (i, 29, 36), is that they are a company united by the fact of their discipleship. Here are Peter and the sons of Zebedee, as of old; one of the two unnamed is likely to have been Andrew; that makes the old quartet (*St. Mark* i, 16-19). But now there are also

Thomas and Nathanael. There is nothing to do but return to the old occupations. Simon Peter, as so often, takes the lead. The word he uses is that which we have often translated " go his way ". It expresses a completely voluntary and self-chosen action; it may be used of wilful choice or the fulfilment of a destiny, but it suggests that the " going " is an individual act; *I am going off to fish*. The others at once decide to join: *We too are coming with thee*. So they go on their self-chosen occupation — innocent, but self-chosen. Night was the best time for fishing; but *in that night they caught nothing*. The work which we do at the impulse of our own wills is futile.

*

(ii) *At the Lord's Command*

4-11. But when dawn was now breaking, there stood Jesus on the beach; howbeit the disciples did not know that it was Jesus. So Jesus saith to them, " Children, have ye any meat? " They answered him " No ". But he said to them " Cast the net on the right side of the ship and ye will find ". So they cast, and no longer had they strength to draw it for the multitude of the fishes. So that disciple whom Jesus loved saith to Peter " It is the Lord ". So Simon Peter, having heard that it was the Lord, girt on his coat, for he was naked, and cast himself into the sea. But the other disciples came in the dinghy (for they were not far from the land but about two hundred cubits) towing the net full of fishes. As soon then as they disembarked on to the land, they see a charcoal-fire laid and fish laid thereon and bread. Jesus saith to them " Bring of the fish which ye caught just now ". So Peter went aboard and drew the net to the land full of great fishes, a hundred and fifty three. And though there were so many, the net did not break.

All *that night* they had toiled in vain. But when the early glimmer of dawn appears, they see a figure standing on the beach. It is still too dark for recognition. He hails them as any casual passer-by might do. I have kept in the translation the words of the Revised Version, *Children, have ye any meat?* But I have done this only because I cannot find a phrase which really gives the sense without falling below the dignity of the whole narrative. Bernard offers, "Boys, you have not had any catch, have you?" which is exactly right in content but jars somewhat in tone. Anyhow, it is no more than a casual, friendly greeting, which does not in the least disclose the identity of the Speaker.

So often the message of the Lord reaches us through some experience or acquaintance reckoned at the time as ordinary and commonplace. Only afterwards, and in the light of results, do we realise what or who was really in touch with us through the apparently common-place event or person.

When the disciples answer *No*, the Stranger's voice is heard giving a command or direction: *Cast the net on the right side of the ship and ye will find*. Advice so definite must represent knowledge, whencesoever derived; *so they cast, and no longer had they strength to draw it for the multitude of the fishes*. What is done in obedience to the Lord's command, even though He who gives the command is not recognised, results in overwhelming success.

Something convinces the Beloved Disciple, one of *the sons of Zebedee* (2), that the Stranger is the Lord. It is idle to speculate how he reached his conviction, but we notice that he who first believed the evidence of the Resurrection at the tomb (xx, 8) is he who first recognises the Lord in the figure dimly seen upon the beach. Simon Peter with characteristic impetuosity, seizes his coat and fastens it around his body, which he had stripped for working the boat and the nets, and casts himself into the sea to hurry to the shore. The other disciples, abandoning the effort to draw up their teeming net into the boat, get into the dinghy and tow the net to shore.

On arriving they find that somehow provision has been made already (9). But Jesus bids them bring of the newly caught fish; so Peter gets into the dinghy where it is beached and drags the net, now attached to its stern, to dry land. They count the fish according to custom — *a hundred and fifty three*. It is perverse to seek a hidden meaning in the number; it is recorded because it was found to be the number when the count was made. Yet *the net did not break*. The gift of God is always more than we can receive yet it never bursts the vessel which we can offer for its reception.

*

(b) The Lord's Gift of Sustenance

12-14. Jesus saith to them " Come and break your fast ". None of the disciples was bold to examine him " Thou — who art thou? " knowing that it was the Lord. Jesus cometh and taketh the bread and giveth to them, and the fish likewise. This is already the third manifestation of Jesus to the disciples after he was raised from the dead.

When His disciples have obeyed His command, the Lord Himself offers them refreshment and sustenance. By this time none is eager to ask the Stranger who He is or to demand His authority for giving them orders. (The word for " ask " or " examine " implies cross-examination or searching enquiry.) They know it is their Lord, and awe in His presence keeps them silent. The Lord again, as of old, is their host. It is strongly suggested that the meal he offers consists partly of what He had himself prepared and partly of what the disciples have brought to land. If so, the symbolism is true. The Lord refreshes us for His service by a gift which is in part derived from Him, in part the fruit of our own labour under His direction; but it is all His gift, for the whole fruit of our labour is His, not our own, and we only enjoy it rightly or fully when we accept it as from Him.

This is *the third manifestation*, that is, the third occasion on which the Lord was manifested; the first was Easter Day when he was manifested at the tomb (xx, 14-17), at Emmaus (*St. Luke* xxiv. 13-31), to Simon Peter (*St. Luke* xxiv, 34), to the assembled disciples (xx, 19-23). The second was a week later (xx, 24-29). This is the third. And this time St. Peter's failure will be recalled and his commission renewed.

*

(2) The Lord and Individual Disciples (15-23)

(a) The Restoration of St. Peter

Before we consider the scene of St. Peter's restoration, let us recall his history as a disciple up to this point as the Evangelists, and especially St. John, bring it before us.

He did not find his own way to the Lord, nor did the Lord directly call him. He was brought by his brother Andrew. The Lord greeted him with the words *Thou art Simon son of John; thou shall be called Rock-man* (i, 42). Rock-man was the most unsuitable name for Simon as he was at that time. *Thou art Simon;* you are our friend called Simon, whom we all know as a loyal, generous, impulsive and unreliable man. *Thou shalt be called Rock-man;* one day — not at once, but in the future — he will earn a title which speaks of strength exactly at what was his weakest point.

From that day, no doubt, Peter was a disciple, but had not yet been called to leave his livelihood to follow his Master. That came later, and the readiness with which he and others responded to the call, " Come ye after me, and I will make you to become fishers of men " (*St. Mark* i, 17, 18) is accounted for by the earlier call and the phase of discipleship which it inaugurated.

After the difficult discourse on the Bread of Life, when *many of the disciples went back and walked no more with him,* and the Lord said to the Twelve *Do ye also want to go?* it was Peter who rallied them with the declaration, *Lord, to whom shall we go? Words of eternal Life hast thou* (vi, 67, 68).

Then there is the scene at Caesarea Philippi. In answer to the question " Who say ye that I am? " Peter answers " Thou art the Christ" (*St. Mark* viii, 29). This draws the declaration from the Lord that he has earned his new name: " Thou art Rock-man, and on this rock I will build my Church " (*St. Matthew* xvi, 18). The quality which will turn Peter's weakness into strength is that on which the Church is to rest — the faith that Jesus is the Christ of God. But when the Lord goes on to say what manner of Christ He will be — " the Son of Man must suffer " — " Peter took him and began to rebuke him " (*St. Mark* viii, 32). It seems incredible. He has just hailed his Master as the Christ of God; and he " took him and began to rebuke him ". Peter acknowledges his Master as Christ, but the very quality of his loyalty leads him to protest against this notion of " a Messiah on a cross " (*I Corinthians* i, 23). He will honour and follow his Lord; but that Lord must so behave as to deserve his honour! Deep in Peter's loyalty is a vein of self-will.

It is sadly easy for passionate loyalty to have this defect — a mortal defect, for it earns from the Lord the name of Satan (*St. Mark* viii, 33). Our passions are mostly egoistic if they rise to the fully personal level at all; the greater part of them are uncontrolled animality. But love and loyalty are personal; and when these are passionate they are as a rule possessive or self-assertive in some degree. We all need urgently the warning of Peter's failure at this point.

We find the same quality at the scene of the Feet-washing (xiii, 1-10). At first Peter wishes to refuse the service which the Lord offers. His loyalty protests. Then when he is told *If I wash thee not, thou hast no part with me* he wants more than was offered: *not my feet only, but also my hands and my head.* Loyal, yes; generous, yes; but submissive, no. The one thing he cannot do is leave the Lord alone to do what He wants. It is this same self-will at the heart of his loyalty that will lead to his great failure.

Then comes the prediction of the desertion of all the disciples. Peter is vehement; whatever others may do, he will not fail. " Although all shall be offended, yet will not I " (*St. Mark* xiv, 29). *My life for thee I will lay down* (xiii, 37). It was true. He was ready to fight for his Master when fighting meant certain death (xviii, 10). But another test awaited him, when there would be no thrill of adventure, no hot blood, but a chill atmosphere, a mocking maid-servant, a jeering crowd — at the hour of cock-crowing. What happened then has not yet been wiped out.

*

15-19. So when the breakfast was over, Jesus saith to Simon Peter, " Simon, son of John, lovest thou me more than these? " He saith to him " Yea, Lord, thou knowest that I am thy friend ". He saith to him " Feed my lambs ". He saith to him again, a second time, " Simon, son of John, lovest thou me? " He saith to him " Yea, Lord, thou knowest that I am thy friend ". He saith to him " Tend my sheep ". He saith to him the third time " Simon, son of John, art thou my friend? " Grieved was Peter because he said to him the third time " Art thou my friend? " And he said to him " Lord, all things thou knowest; thou seest that I am thy friend ". Jesus saith to him " Feed my sheep. Amen, Amen I say to thee, when thou wast younger, thou girdedst thyself and walkedst where thou wouldest; but when thou art grown old, thou shalt stretch forth thy hands, and another will gird thee and carry thee where thou wouldest not." — (And this he said signifying by what manner of death he should glorify God; and having said this he saith to him) — " Follow me ".[1]

---

[1] Some scholars have urged that there is no distinction to be drawn between the two words for " love ". Thus Bernard gives a whole list of passages where they are interchangeable. For myself I do not believe that any two words ever have precisely the same meaning; there is always some difference of tone or suggestion. But, whether that is so or not, in the passages quoted by Bernard one or the other of the two words occurs alone, not both together. It is not reasonably conceivable that both should be used together, and that with an alternation which challenges attention,

The Lord has by a " sign " illustrated the blessing which rests on work done in obedience to His command. He has refreshed His friends with sustenance which is, in part, the product of their own labour. Then He turns to the eager-hearted follower whose loyalty so sadly failed as a result of the self-will that was intermingled with it. He had once said, "Although all shall be offended, yet will not I "; he had claimed a devotion more sure than that of his fellow-disciples. Does he claim that still? *Simon, son of John, lovest thou me more than these?* Peter says nothing of the comparison with others; on that score he can make no claim. Nor does he claim to love his Lord with that self-forgetful love which Christ had made known to men and to stand for which the Greek word — Agapē — had been drawn out of its commonplace obscurity. Human love is a tainted thing, tinged with lust or with the possessiveness which is self-will and is the spring of jealousy. The words commonly used for love are not free from those associations. So this word which had no bad suggestiveness because it had none at all was used to stand for the pure and holy love of God as Christ disclosed it, to gather from that disclosure its associations and suggestions. Peter will not use which word of himself; he uses the word of simple friendship; *Yea, Lord, thou knowest that I am thy friend.* That at least, in spite of everything, he can claim. Because he can make that claim, the commission can be given : *Feed my lambs.*

if their meaning is quite the same. Andrew Bradley remarks that for many purposes the two words " steed " and " horse " mean the same thing; but if they are used together, their difference becomes evident, and to transpose them may have a ludicrous result: e.g.

> " Bring forth the steed." The steed was brought.
> In truth he was a noble horse.

So it may be with the two words used here. I have alluded to the distinction in commenting on xvi, 27. But while I think the distinction is relevant there, where only one word is used, I have no doubt about it here where both are used.

Then the Lord repeats the question, but this time without any addition of comparisons. Whether more or less than others, does Peter love his Lord? *Simon, son of John, lovest thou me?* Peter still gives the same answer: *Yea, Lord, thou knowest that I am thy friend.* And again the commission is given: *Tend my sheep.*

Once more the Lord questions Peter, and this time he changes the form of question and adopts Peter's own word: *Simon, son of John, art thou my friend?* Is even that true? Peter was grieved, not only because, recalling the threefold denial, the Lord puts His question for the third time, but also because this time He questions even that lesser claim which Peter had made. He pleads not only the Lord's unerring knowledge of what is in him, but his own manifest sincerity: *Lord, thou knowest all things; thou seest that I am thy friend.*

Thou seest; elsewhere I have translated this Greek word " recognise ". In the other two answers, and here in the first phrase, Peter uses the word that stands for knowledge of facts or truths; here he uses the word for acquaintance and appreciation. Before the Lord is His devoted, loyal and deeply penitent disciple: *thou seest that I am thy friend.*

We too have often failed our Lord; we stand before Him ashamed and penitent. Can we say with Peter's confidence *Thou seest that I am thy friend?* If we can, the commission to do the Lord's work may be given to us. We may not be able to say that we love Him with love like that which He has shewn to us; but we must be able to say " I am thy friend ". We must have taken our stand on His side, with full intention to be constant in our devotion. We may fail through weakness; but if that be all we shall hear Him saying, *Let not your hearts be troubled. Trust God and trust me* (xiv, 1). If we can sincerely say we are His friends, He is ready to let us serve Him by serving His people.

The Lord's questions follow a declining scale:

Lovest thou me more than these? — Lovest thou me? — Art thou my friend? But the commissions follow an ascending scale: *Feed my lambs — Tend my sheep — Feed my sheep.* The change of expression shews that some change of meaning is intended. *Feed my lambs:* the first charge is to supply the needs of the young of the flock — a task of infinite responsibility, but not, as spiritual work is reckoned, conspicuously difficult, for the lambs are ready to accept the sustenance offered to them. *Tend my sheep:* the second charge is to exercise general guidance of the flock, including its mature members, a task for one of greater experience than the first. *Feed my sheep:* the third charge is the hardest — to supply the needs of the mature members of the flock; for it is less easy to discern their needs than those of the " lambs ", and they often have no knowledge of what their own needs are, or, still worse, suppose that they know when in fact they do not.

My sheep. The words come back to mind: — *The sheep hear his voice, and his own sheep he calleth by name and leadeth them out . . . the sheep follow him because they know his voice. But a stranger will they not follow, but will flee from him, because they do not know the voice of strangers . . . the sheep that are mine hear my voice, and I know them, and they follow me* (x, 3, 4, 5, 27). Whether we seem to His sheep their shepherds or strangers will depend on whether they can recognise our voice as His; and this in turn will depend on the reality of our claim — *thou knowest that I am thy friend.*

Once more the familiar and solemn words are used *Amen, Amen I say to thee.* When they were last spoken to Peter they heralded the prediction of his denial (xiii, 38). Now they herald the prediction of his martyrdom. Once Peter had been wilful and head-strong. His impulses were generous, but he followed them as much because they were his as because they were generous. He chose his own path and walked

where he would. As the ardour of youth cools and
the feebleness of age comes on, all this will change.
He will stretch forth his hands as he gropes along
unknown ways, and others will carry him against his
choice. The words as spoken foreshadow a compulsion
laid upon him, but not necessarily more than this.
The Evangelist, writing with St. Peter's martyrdom
in mind, sees in them a direct reference to it. For St.
Peter's hands, like those of his Lord, were stretched
out upon a cross. *When thou shalt be old, thou shalt
stretch forth thy hands, and another will gird thee and
carry thee where thou wouldest not. Follow me.*

Follow me. A few days before the Lord had said
*Whither I go thou canst not follow me now, but thou
shalt follow afterwards* (xiii, 36). Now he says *Follow
me.* For it is possible now. The outward presence of
the Lord is being withdrawn; the power of the Holy
Spirit is given and will soon take possession; Peter,
reckless and cowardly by turns, fighting in the garden
but denying in the High Priest's court, will stand forth
before the rulers of his people in the serenity of imper-
turbable courage — Rock-man indeed.

Yet it is with reference, not to what he will do, but
to what others will do to him, that the Lord says with
so solemn an emphasis *Follow me.* (Is it not true that
in a certain deep sense nothing which the Lord did
was so important as what others did to Him? No
doubt His endurance is what gave its quality to the
event; but His passivity is more powerful than His
acts. He reigns from the Tree.) Will Peter follow
to the end?

Yes, to the very bitter end; yet even so, if the
legend is trustworthy, there lingered to the end some
of the old weakness which makes Peter so unfailing a
spring of encouragement to most of us. The example
of Paul is of little use to me; I am not a hero. The
example of John is of but little more use; my love
is so feeble. But Peter is a source of constant

encouragement, for his weakness is so manifest, yet because he was truly the friend of his Lord he became the Prince of the Apostles and glorified God by his death.

The story tells how Peter escaped from his Roman prison the night before his martyrdom and was fleeing along the Appian Way when he met a familiar Figure bearing a cross. *"Domine, quo vadis?"*—"Lord, whither goest thou?" "I am going to Rome to be crucified afresh." Peter turned and was found in his prison when the guards came for him in the morning. History or legend? We do not know. If history, then fact or dream? We do not know. The story shows that the early Church thought of Peter as still shewing to the end some of the weakness of Simon, son of John; but the love of the Lord led him captive at the last.

*

(b) The Vocation of St. John

St. Peter has received his commission and his call; it is a call to follow by difficult stages to the complete offering of the will that was by nature so self-assertive. Close beside the Lord is the Beloved Disciple. Is there any call for him? The Lord, it would seem, has illustrated the command *Follow me* by the gesture of moving away from the main body of the disciples, and as Peter followed, the Beloved Disciple moved with him. So Peter turns to " follow ", and his attention is caught by the presence of this one of all their company whom they knew to be the most intimate.

20-23. Turning about, Peter seeth the disciple whom Jesus loved following — who also leaned back on his breast at the supper and said " Lord, who is it that is betraying thee? " So having seen him Peter saith to Jesus " Lord, this man, what of him? " Jesus saith to him " If I will that he abide while I am coming, what is that to thee ? Do thou follow me." So this saying went forth among the

brethren that that disciple would not die. Yet Jesus did not say to
him that he would not die, but " If I will that he abide while I am
coming what is that to thee? "

As the Lord moves, the Beloved Disciple has moved
too; it was natural that one so intimate as the incident
at the Last Supper proves him to have been, should
keep close to his Master without any special command.
But Peter's curiosity is aroused. His own future has
been declared; what of John's?

The Lord does not answer speculative questions or
satisfy curiosity. To the question " Are they few that
be saved? " His answer was " Strive to enter it by
the narrow door " (*St. Luke* xiii, 23). So when St.
Peter asks about the future in store for his fellow-
disciple, the reply is *If I will that he abide while I am
coming, what is that to thee? Do thou follow me.* Our
duty is to obey, without waiting to know what orders
or promises may be given to others.

Incidentally the recalling of this episode makes it
possible to explain and dissipate the rumour that St.
John would survive till the expected Second Coming.
Nothing of the kind had been promised. All that was
said was that even if this were the Lord's intention for
St. John, this was no business of St. Peter's; his business was plain: *Do thou follow me.*

Abide while I am coming. This translation exaggerates the suggestion of the original, but the suggestion is there. The Coming of the Lord is, from the
time of the Passion, permanent present fact. " He
cometh with the clouds "; that is present. " Every
eye shall see him "; that is future.

So the story of this Gospel ends with a little group
standing apart from the company of the disciples. It
consists of three: the Lord of love; the disciple in
whom self would be offered; and the disciple in whom
self would be forgotten.

If we are to enter into the Life to which the Lord
Jesus invites us, the self in us must be eliminated as a

factor in the determination of conduct; if possible, let
it be so effaced by love that it is forgotten; if that may
not be, let it be offered. For if we are to *come to the
Father*, self must be either offered or forgotten.

*

POSTSCRIPT

(3) THE FINAL TESTIMONY

The Gospel proper is ended. The Evangelist,
whom we take to be John the Elder, an intimate
disciple of John the Apostle, adds a brief note of testimony to the reliability of John the Apostle's witness,
which lies behind this Gospel.

24, 25. This is the disciple who bears witness of these things and who
wrote these things, and we know that his witness is true. And there
are also other things which Jesus did, the which, if they should be
written every one, I suppose that even the world itself would not
contain the books written.

This is the disciple who bears witness of these things:
so the Beloved Disciple is still living when the Elder
composes the Gospel. *And who wrote these things*; he
is the real author; and very likely himself wrote or
dictated parts of what is presented in the Gospel. *We
know that his witness is true.* The Elder could say this
because he knew his teacher, and because he had tested
and proved his witness, probably by comparison with
the witness of others, certainly by the test of life
and of spiritual communion with the crucified and
risen Lord.

It is only part of the story that is here set forth,
as was said at the close of the Gospel as first planned
(see xx, 30, 31). Now the Elder, who has written till
these closing sentences under the direct influence of
the Apostle and has handled the sublimest themes
with severe and unbroken restraint, permits himself one

touch of hyperbole: for to tell the whole story of Jesus' love and power would exhaust the capacities of the universe.

O Lord Jesus Christ, thou Word and Revelation of the Eternal Father, come, we pray thee, take possession of our hearts and reign where thou hast right to reign. So fill our minds with the thought and our imaginations with the picture of thy love, that there may be in us no room for any desire that is discordant with thy holy will. Cleanse us, we pray thee, from all that may make us deaf to thy call or slow to obey it, who, with the Father and the Holy Spirit art one God, blessed for ever. Amen.

THE END

Printed in Great Britain by R. & R. CLARK, LIMITED, Edinburgh.